ANCIENT WISDOM, MODERN WORLD

Ethics for a New Millennium

Also by His Holiness the Dalai Lama

Freedom in Exile

ANCIENT WISDOM, MODERN WORLD

Ethics for a New Millennium

Tenzin Gyatso
His Holiness the Dalai Lama

LITTLE, BROWN AND COMPANY

A *Little, Brown* Book

First published in Great Britain by
Little, Brown and Company 1999

Copyright © Tenzin Gyatso, the Fourteenth Dalai Lama
of Tibet, 1999

The moral right of the author has been asserted.

A CIP catalogue record for this book
is available from the British Library.

ISBN 0 316 91428 2

Typeset in Weiss by
Palimpsest Book Production Limited,
Polmont, Stirlingshire
Printed and bound in Great Britain by
Creative Print and Design, Ebbw Vale, Wales

Little, Brown and Company (UK)
Brettenham House
Lancaster Place
London WC2E 7EN

CONTENTS

Introduction and Acknowledgements   vii

PART ONE – THE FOUNDATIONS OF ETHICS

1 Modern Society and the Quest for Human
   Happiness   3
2 No Magic, No Mystery   19
3 Dependent Origination and the Nature of Reality   35
4 Redefining the Goal   51
5 Nying-je, The Supreme Emotion   67

PART TWO – ETHICS AND THE INDIVIDUAL

6 The Ethics of Restraint   85
7 The Ethics of Virtue   107
8 The Ethics of Compassion   131
9 Ethics and Suffering   141
10 The Need for Discernment   153

PART THREE — ETHICS AND SOCIETY

11 Universal Responsibility   169
12 Levels of Commitment   181
13 Peace and Disarmament   187
14 Further Responsibilities   205
15 The Role of Religion in Modern Society   227
   An Appeal   241

INTRODUCTION AND ACKNOWLEDGEMENTS

Having lost my country at the age of sixteen and become a refugee at twenty-four, I have faced a great many difficulties during the course of my life. When I consider them, I see that many were insurmountable. Not only were they unavoidable, but they were incapable of favourable resolution. Nonetheless, in terms of my own peace of mind and physical health, I can claim to have coped reasonably well. As a result I have been able to meet adversity with all my resources – mental, physical and spiritual. I could not have done so if I had been overwhelmed by anxiety and despair. My health would have been harmed. I would also have been constrained in my actions.

Yet as I look around, I see that it is not only we Tibetan refugees and members of other displaced communities who face difficulties. Everywhere and in every society, people endure suffering and adversity – even those who enjoy freedom and material prosperity. Moreover, it occurs to me that much of the unhappiness we humans endure is actually of our own making. In principle, therefore, this at least is avoidable. I also see that, generally, those individuals whose conduct is ethically positive are happier and find more meaning in life than those who neglect ethics. This confirms my belief that if we can re-orientate our thoughts and emotions, and reorder our behaviour, not only can we learn to cope with suffering more easily, but we can prevent a great deal of it from arising in the first place.

What I mean by the term positive ethical conduct I shall try to show in this book. In doing so, I acknowledge that it is very difficult either to generalize successfully or to be absolutely precise about ethics and morality. Rarely, if ever, is any situation totally black and white. The same act will have different shades and degrees of moral value under different circumstances. At the same time, it is essential that we reach a consensus in respect of what constitutes positive conduct and what constitutes negative conduct, what is right and what is wrong, what is appropriate and what is inappropriate. In the past, the respect people had for religion meant that ethical practice was maintained through a majority following one religion or another. But this is no longer the case. We must therefore find some other way of establishing basic ethical principles.

Not that the reader should suppose that, as Dalai Lama, I have any special solution to offer. There is nothing in these pages which has not been said before. Indeed, I feel that the concerns and ideas expressed here are shared by many of those who think about and attempt to find solutions to the problems and suffering we humans face. In responding to the suggestion of some of my friends and offering this book to the public, my hope is to give voice to those millions who, not having an opportunity to articulate their views in public, remain members of what I take to be a silent majority.

The reader should, however, bear in mind that my formal learning has been of an entirely religious and spiritual character. Since my youth, my chief (and continuing) field of study has been Buddhist philosophy and psychology. In particular, I have studied the works of the religious philosophers of the Geluk school to which the Dalai Lamas have traditionally belonged. Being a firm believer in religious pluralism, I have also studied the principal works of other Buddhist traditions. I have had comparatively little exposure to modern, secular, thought. Yet this is not a religious book. Still less is it a book about Buddhism. My aim has been to appeal for an approach to ethics based on universal rather than religious principles.

As a result, producing a work for a general audience has not been without challenges and it is the result of teamwork. One particular difficulty arose from the fact that it is difficult to render into modern language a number of the Tibetan terms it seemed essential to use. I have tried to explain these in such a way that they could be understood readily by a non-specialist readership and also rendered clearly into other languages. But in doing so, and in trying to communicate unambiguously with readers whose language and culture may be quite different from my own, it is possible that some shades of meaning in the Tibetan have been lost and others have been added unintentionally. I trust that careful editing has minimized this. Where any such distortions come to light, I would hope to correct them in a subsequent edition. In the meantime, for his assistance in this area, for his translation into English and for innumerable suggestions, I wish to thank Dr TJ Langri. I wish also to thank Mr AR Norman for his work of redaction. This has been invaluable. Finally, I would like to record my thanks to those others who have helped bring this work to fruition.

Dharamsala, February 1999

PART ONE

The Foundations of Ethics

MODERN SOCIETY AND THE QUEST FOR HUMAN HAPPINESS

I am a comparative newcomer to the modern world. Although I fled my homeland as long ago as 1959, and although my life since then as a refugee in India has brought me into much closer contact with contemporary society, my formative years were spent largely cut off from the realities of the twentieth century. This was partly due to my appointment as Dalai Lama: I became a monk at a very early age. It also reflects the fact that we Tibetans had chosen – mistakenly in my view – to remain isolated behind the high mountain ranges which separate our country from the rest of the world. Today, however, I travel a great deal, both at home and abroad, and it is my good fortune to be meeting new people continually.

Many people, especially those who make the effort to travel to the Indian hill-station at Dharamsala where I live in exile, come to me seeking something. Amongst them are some who have suffered greatly. There are those who have lost parents and children. There are those with friends or family who have committed suicide. There are those who are sick with cancer and with AIDS related illnesses. Then, of course, there are fellow Tibetans with their own tragedies of hardship and suffering. Some of these people have unrealistic expectations. They assume that I have healing powers or that I can give some sort of blessing. But I am only an ordinary human being. The best I can do is try to help them by sharing in their suffering.

For my own part, meeting innumerable people from all over the world and from every walk of life reminds me of our basic sameness as human beings. Indeed, the more I see of the world, the clearer it becomes that, no matter what our situation, whether we are rich or poor, educated or not, of one race, gender, religion or another, we all desire to be happy and to avoid suffering. Our every intended action, in a sense our whole life – how we choose to live it within the context of the limitations imposed by our circumstances – can be seen as our answer to the great question which confronts us all: 'How am I to be happy?'

We are sustained in our quest for happiness, it seems to me, by hope. We know, even if we do not admit it, that there can be no guarantee of a better, happier life than the one we are leading today. As an old Tibetan proverb puts it, 'the next life or tomorrow – we can never be certain which will come first.' But we hope to go on living. We hope that through this or that action we can bring about happiness. Everything we do, not only as individuals but also at the level of society, can be seen in terms of this fundamental aspiration. Indeed, it is one shared by all sentient beings. As such it needs no justification. The desire or inclination to be happy and to avoid suffering knows no boundaries. It is in our nature.

And this is precisely what we see in countries both rich and poor. Everywhere, by all means imaginable, people are striving to improve their lives. Yet strangely, my impression is that those living in the materially developed countries are in some ways less satisfied despite their industry. They are less happy and to some extent suffer more than those living in the least developed countries. Indeed, if we compare the rich with those who are poor, it often seems that those with nothing are in fact those with the least anxiety, though they may be plagued with physical pains and suffering. As for the rich, whilst a few know how to use their wealth intelligently – that is to say not in luxurious living but sharing it with the needy – most do not. Many are so caught up with the idea of acquiring still more that they make no room for anything else in their lives. In their absorption they actually lose the dream of happiness which riches were to have provided. As a result, they are constantly torn between doubt about what might happen and the hope of gaining more. They are plagued with mental and emotional suffering – even though they may outwardly appear to be leading entirely successful and comfortable lives. This is evident in the disturbing prevalence of anxiety, discontent, frustration, uncertainty, doubt and depression amongst the populations of the materially developed countries. To my mind, such inner suffering clearly reflects a growing confusion in respect of what morality consists in and what its foundations are.

I am often put in mind of this paradox when I go abroad. It frequently happens when I arrive in a new country that at first everything seems very pleasant, very beautiful. Everybody I meet is very friendly. There is nothing to complain about. But then, day by day, I begin to hear about people's problems, their concerns and worries. Below the surface, so many feel uneasy and dissatisfied with their lives. They experience feelings of isolation; then depression follows. The result is the troubled atmosphere which is such a feature of the developed world.

At first this surprised me. Although I never imagined that material wealth alone could overcome suffering, still, looking towards the developed world from Tibet, a country then as now very poor in this respect, I must admit that I thought it must go further towards doing so than is the case. I expected that, with physical suffering much reduced, as it is for the majority living in the industrially developed countries, happiness would be much easier to achieve than for those living under more severe conditions.

Instead, the extraordinary advancements of science and technology seem to have achieved little more than linear improvement. In many cases, progress has meant little more than greater numbers of opulent houses in more cities with more cars driving between them. Certainly there has been a reduction in some types of suffering especially certain illnesses. But there has been no overall reduction.

Saying this, I remember well an occasion on one of my early trips to the West. I was the guest of a very wealthy family which lived in a large, well-appointed house. Everyone was very charming and polite. There were servants to cater to one's every need and I began to think that here, perhaps, was proof positive that wealth could be a source of happiness. My hosts definitely had an air of relaxed confidence. When I subsequently saw an array of tranquillizers and sleeping pills in the bathroom, through a cupboard door which was slightly open, I was forcefully reminded that there is often a big gap between outward appearances and inner reality.

This paradox whereby inner – or we could say psycho-logical and emotional – suffering is so often to be found amidst material wealth is readily apparent throughout much of the West. Indeed, it is so pervasive that we might wonder whether there is something in Western culture which predisposes people living there to such kinds of suffering? This I doubt. So many factors are involved. Clearly material development itself has a role to play. But we can also cite the increasing urbanization of modern society where high concentrations of people live in close proximity to one another. In this context, consider that in place of our dependence on one another for support, today wherever possible, we tend to rely on machines and services. Whereas formerly, farmers would call in all their family members to help with the harvest, today they simply telephone a contractor. We find modern living so organized as to demand the least possible practical dependence on others. The more or less universal ambition seems to be for everyone to own his or her own house, their own car, their own computer and so on in order to be as independent as possible. We can also point to the increasing autonomy that people enjoy as a result of advances in science and technology. It is possible today to be far more independent of others than ever before. There has arisen a sense that our future is not dependent on our neighbours but rather on our jobs, or on our employers. This in turn encourages us to assume that others are not important for our happiness, therefore, their happiness is unimportant.

As a result, we have created a society in which people

find it harder and harder to show one another basic affection. In place of the sense of community and belonging,
which we find such a reassuring feature of less wealthy
and generally rural societies, we find a high degree of
loneliness and alienation. Despite the fact that millions
live in close proximity to one another, it seems that many
people, especially the old, have no one to talk to but their
pets. I often think of modern industrial society in terms of
a huge self-propelled machine. Instead of human beings in
charge, each individual is a tiny, insignificant component
with no choice but to move when the machine moves.

All this is compounded by the contemporary rhetoric of
growth and economic development. This often reinforces
the tendency towards competitiveness and envy. And with
this comes the perceived need to keep up appearances
– itself a major source of problems, tension and unhappiness. The psychological and emotional suffering we
find so prevalent in the West is therefore less likely to
reflect a cultural shortcoming than an underlying human
tendency. Actually, I have noticed that this inner suffering
is beginning to manifest outside the West. In some parts
of South-East Asia, it is observable that traditional belief
systems have begun to lose their influence over people as
affluence increases. The result is that we find a broadly
similar manifestation of unease as that established in the
West. This suggests that the potential exists in us all,
and in the same way that physical disease reflects its
environment, so it is with psychological and emotional

suffering. It arises within the context of particular circumstances. Thus, in the Southern, undeveloped countries we find ailments, such as those arising from poor sanitation, broadly confined to that part of the world. In urban industrial societies, illness also manifests itself in ways that are consistent with the environment. Instead of water-borne diseases, we find stress-related illness. All this implies that there are strong reasons to assume a link exists between our disproportionate emphasis on external progress and the unhappiness, the anxiety, and the lack of contentment in modern society.

This may sound a very gloomy assessment. But unless we acknowledge the extent and character of our problems, we will not be able even to begin to overcome them. Nor will we be able to resolve them until we address their underlying causes and seek their origin. Clearly a major reason for modern society's devotion to material progress is the very success of science and technology. Now the wonderful thing about these forms of human endeavour is that they bring immediate satisfaction. They're unlike prayer, the results of which are for the most part invisible – if indeed it works at all. And we are impressed by results. What could be more normal? Unfortunately, this devotion encourages us to suppose that the keys to happiness are material well-being on the one hand and the power conferred by knowledge on the other. Whilst it is obvious to anyone who gives this mature thought that material well-being cannot bring us happiness by itself, it may be less apparent that knowledge cannot. But mere knowledge cannot provide the happiness that springs from inner development. Indeed, though our very detailed and specific knowledge of external phenomena is an immense achievement, the urge to reduce, to narrow down in pursuit of them, far from bringing us happiness can actually be dangerous. It can cause us to lose touch with the wider reality of human experience and in particular our dependence on others.

We need also to recognize what happens when we rely too much on the external achievements of science. For example, as the influence of religion declines, confusion mounts with respect to the problem of how best to conduct ourselves in life. In the past, religion and ethics were closely intertwined. Now many people believe that science has 'disproven' religion. They make the further assumption that, because there is no final evidence for any spiritual authority, morality itself must be a matter of individual preference. It seems that in the past scientists and philosophers felt a pressing need to find solid foundations on which to establish immutable laws and absolute truths. Nowadays, this kind of research is held to be futile. As a result, we see a complete reversal, heading off towards another extreme in which reality itself is called into question. This can only lead to chaos.

In saying this, I do not mean to criticize scientific endeavour. I have learned a great deal from my encounters with scientists and I see no obstacle to engaging in dialogue with them even when their perspective is one of radical materialism. Indeed, for as long as I can remember, I have been fascinated by the insights of science. As a boy there was a time when I was rather more interested in learning about the mechanics of an old film projector I found in the storerooms of the Norbulingka, the summer residence of the Dalai Lama, than in my religious and scholastic studies. My concern is rather that we are apt to overlook the limitations of science narrowly defined. By replacing religion as the final source of knowledge in popular estimation, science begins to look a bit like another religion itself. With this comes the danger of blind faith in its principles and a corresponding intolerance of alternate views on the part of some of its adherents. That this supplanting of religion has taken place is not surprising given the extraordinary achievements of science. Who could fail to be impressed at our ability to land people on the moon? Yet the fact remains that if we were to go to, a nuclear physicist and say: 'I am facing a moral dilemma, what should I do?' He or she could only suggest we look elsewhere for an answer.

Generally speaking, a scientist is in no better a position than a lawyer in this respect. Whilst both science and the law can help us forecast the likely consequence of our actions, neither can tell us how we ought to act in a moral sense. Moreover, we need to recognize the limits of scientific enquiry itself with respect to human consciousness. For example, though we have been aware of consciousness throughout history, scientists still do not understand what it actually is, nor why it exists, how it functions or what its essential nature is though it has been the subject of investigation for millennia. Science can neither tell us what the substantial cause of consciousness is, nor what its effects are. Of course, consciousness belongs to that category of phenomena without form, substance or colour. It is not susceptible to investigation by external means. But this does not mean such things do not exist, merely that science cannot find them.

Should we, therefore, abandon scientific enquiry on the grounds that it has failed us? Certainly not. Nor do I believe that the goal of prosperity for all is not entirely valid. Because of our nature, bodily and physical experience plays a dominant role in our lives. The achievements of science and technology clearly reflect our desire to attain a better, more comfortable existence. This is very good. Who could fail to applaud the eradication of certain diseases? At the same time, I think it is genuinely true that members of certain traditional, rural communities do enjoy greater harmony and tranquillity than those settled in our modern cities. For example, in the Spiti area of northern India, it remains the custom for locals not to lock their houses when they go out. It is expected that a visitor finding the house empty would go in and help themselves to a meal whilst waiting for the family to return. The same custom obtained in Tibet in former times. This is not to say that there is no crime in such places. In Tibet such things did happen occasionally of course. But when they did people raised their eyebrows in surprise. It was a rare and unusual event. By contrast, in some modern cities, it is a remarkable event if a day goes by when there is not a murder.

We must be careful not to idealize old ways of life, however. The high level of cooperation we find in undeveloped rural communities may be based more on necessity than on good will. People recognize it as an alternative to greater hardship. And the contentment we perceive may actually have more to do with ignorance. These people may not realise or imagine that any other way of life is possible. If they did, very likely they would embrace it eagerly. The challenge we face is to find a means of enjoying the same degree of harmony and tranquillity as those more traditional communities whilst participating fully in the realities of the world as we find it at the dawn of a new millennium. To say otherwise is to say that these communities should not even try to improve their standard of living. Yet, I am quite certain that, the majority of Tibet's nomads would be very glad of: the latest thermal clothing for winter; smokeless fuel to cook with; the benefits of modern medicine and a portable television in their tents. And I, for one, would not wish to deny them these things.

Modern society, with all its benefits and defects has

emerged within the context of innumerable causes and conditions. To assume that merely by abandoning material progress we would overcome all our problems is short-sighted. It ignores their underlying causes. Besides, there is still much in the modern world to be optimistic about.

There are countless people even in the most developed countries who are active in their concern for others. Nearer home, I think of the enormous kindness we Tibetan refugees have been shown by those whose personal resources were also quite limited. For example, our children have benefited immeasurably from the selfless contribution of their Indian teachers, many of whom have been compelled to live under difficult conditions far away from their homes. On a wider scale, we might also consider the growing appreciation of fundamental human rights. This represents a very positive development. Generally, the way in which the international community responds to natural disasters with immediate aid is a wonderful feature of the modern world. The increasing recognition that we cannot forever continue to mistreat our natural environment without facing serious consequences is also cause for hope. I also believe that, thanks largely to modern communications, people are probably more accepting of diversity than formerly, and standards of literacy and education throughout the world are higher in general than ever before. I take such positive developments to be an indication of what we humans are capable.

Recently, I had the opportunity to meet the Queen

Mother in England. This gave me great pleasure as she has been a familiar figure to me throughout my life. But what was particularly encouraging was to hear her opinion, as a woman as old as the twentieth century itself, that the world has become much more aware than it was when she was young. In those days, she said, people were interested mainly in their own countries whereas today there is much more concern for others abroad. When I asked her whether she was optimistic for the future, she replied in the affirmative without hesitation.

It is true, of course, that we can point to an abundance of severely negative trends within modern society. There seems little doubt of the escalation in crime rates. Murder, violence, and rape multiply year by year. In addition, we frequently hear of abusive and exploitative relationships both in the home and within the wider community; of growing numbers of young people addicted to drugs and alcohol; and of the effect on children of the high proportion of marriages ending in divorce. Not even our own small refugee community has escaped the impact of some of these developments. Whereas, for example, suicide was almost completely unknown in Tibetan society, lately there have been one or two tragic incidents of this kind. Likewise, whereas drug addiction amongst young Tibetans certainly did not exist a generation ago, we now have a few cases – mainly, it must be said, in those places where they are exposed to the modern urban lifestyle.

Yet, unlike the sufferings of sickness, old age and death, none of these problems are by nature inevitable. Nor are they due to any lack of knowledge. When we think carefully, we see that they are all ethical problems. Each reflects our understanding of what is right and wrong, of what is positive and what is negative, of what is appropriate and what is inappropriate. And beyond this we can point to something more fundamental: a neglect of what I call our inner dimension.

What do I mean by this? Consider our over emphasis on material gain. There is a tendency to assume that, this alone can provide us with all the satisfactions we require. Yet by nature, the satisfactions it can provide will be limited to the level of the physical senses. If it were true that we human beings were no different from animals, this would be fine. However, given the complexity of our species – in particular the fact that we experience thoughts and emotions as well as possess imaginative and critical faculties – it is obvious that our needs transcend the merely sensual. The prevalence of anxiety, stress, doubt, confusion, uncertainty and depression amongst those whose basic needs have been met is a clear indication of this. Our problems, both those we experience externally, such as wars, crime and violence and those we experience internally as emotional and psychological suffering, will not be solved until we address this underlying neglect of our inner dimension. That is why the great movements of the last hundred years and more – democracy, liberalism, socialism and Communism – have all failed to deliver the universal benefits they were supposed to provide, despite many wonderful ideas. A revolution is called for, certainly, but not a political, an economic or a technical revolution. We have had enough experience of these during the past century to know that a purely external approach will not suffice. What I propose is a spiritual revolution.

CHAPTER TWO

NO MAGIC, NO MYSTERY

In calling for a spiritual revolution, am I advocating a religious solution to our problems after all? No. As someone nearing seventy years of age at the time of this writing, I have accumulated enough experience to be completely confident that the teachings of the Buddha are both relevant and useful to humanity. If a person puts them into practice, it is certain that not only they but others too will benefit. My meetings with many different sorts of people the world over have helped me realize that there are other faiths, and other cultures, no less capable than mine of enabling individuals to lead constructive and satisfying lives. What is more, I have come to the conclusion that whether or not a person is a religious believer does not matter much. Far more important is that they be a good human being.

I say this in acknowledgement of the fact that, of the earth's nearly six billion human beings, though a majority may claim allegiance to one faith or another, the influence of religion on people's lives is generally marginal, at least in the developed world. It is doubtful whether, globally, even a billion are what I would call dedicated religious practitioners: people who try, on a daily basis, faithfully to follow the principles and precepts of their faith. The rest remain, in this sense, non-practising. Those who are dedicated practitioners follow a multiplicity of religious paths. From this it becomes clear that given our diversity no single religion satisfies all humanity. We can also conclude that we humans can live quite well without recourse to religious faith.

These may seem unusual statements, coming as they do from a religious figure. I am, however, Tibetan before I am Dalai Lama and I am human before I am Tibetan. So whilst as Dalai Lama I have a special responsibility to Tibetans, and as a monk I have a special responsibility towards furthering interreligious harmony, as a human being I have a much larger responsibility in respect of the whole human family – which indeed we all have. And since the majority does not practise religion, I am concerned with finding a way to serve all humanity without recourse to religious faith.

Actually, I believe that if we consider the world's major religions from the widest perspective, we find that Buddhism, Christianity, Hinduism, Islam, Judaism, Sikhism, Zoroastrianism and all others are directed towards helping human beings achieve lasting happiness. Each of them is, in my opinion, capable of facilitating this. Under such circumstances, a variety of religions – each of which promotes the same basic values after all – is both desirable and useful.

Not that I always felt this. When I was younger and living in Tibet, I believed in my heart that Buddhism was the best way. I told myself it would be marvellous if everyone converted. Yet this was due to ignorance. We Tibetans had, of course, heard of other religions. But what little we knew about them came from Tibetan translations of secondary Buddhist, sources. Naturally, these focussed on those aspects of other religions which are more open to debate from a Buddhist perspective. This was not because their Buddhist authors deliberately wished to caricature their opponents. Rather, it reflected the fact that the authors had no need to recapitulate all the aspects with which they had no argument. In India, where they wrote, the works they were discussing were available in their entirety. Unfortunately this was not the case in Tibet. Translations of these other scriptures were not available to us.

As I grew up, I gradually learned more about the other world religions. Especially after coming into exile, I began to meet people who, having dedicated their entire lives to different faiths – some through prayer and meditation, others through actively serving others – had acquired a profound experience of their particular tradition. Such personal exchanges helped me recognize the enormous value of each of the major faith traditions and led me to respect them deeply. For me, Buddhism remains the most precious path. It corresponds best to my personality. But that does not mean I believe it to be the best religion for everyone, any more than I believe it necessary for everyone to be a religious believer.

Of course, both as a Tibetan and as a monk, I have been brought up according to and educated in the principles, the precepts and the practise of Buddhism. I cannot therefore deny that my whole thinking is shaped by my understanding of what it means to be a follower of the Buddha. However, my concern in this book is to try to reach beyond the formal boundaries of my faith. I want to show that there are grounds for supposing it possible to describe some universal principles which could help everyone to achieve the happiness to which we all aspire. Some people may feel that in this I am attempting to propagate Buddhism by stealth. But whilst it is difficult for me to prove, this is not the case.

Actually, I believe there is an important distinction to be made between religion and spirituality. Religion I take to be concerned with belief in the claims to salvation of one faith tradition or another – an aspect of which is acceptance of some form of metaphysical or supernatural reality, including perhaps an idea of heaven or *nirvana*. Connected with this are religious teachings or dogma, rituals, prayer and so on. Spirituality I take to be concerned with those qualities of the human spirit – such as love and compassion, patience, tolerance, forgiveness, contentment, a sense of responsibility, a sense of harmony – which bring happiness to both self and others. Whilst ritual and prayer, along with the questions of *nirvana* and salvation are directly connected with religious faith, these inner qualities need not be, however. There is thus no reason why the individual should not develop them, even to a high degree, without recourse to any religious or metaphysical belief system. This is why I sometimes say that religion is something we can perhaps do without. What we cannot do without are these basic spiritual qualities.

Those who practise religion would of course be right to say that such qualities, or virtues, are fruits of genuine religious endeavour and, therefore, that religion has everything to do with developing them and with what may be called spiritual practice. But let us be clear on this point. Religious faith demands spiritual practice. Yet it seems there is much confusion, as often amongst religious believers as amongst non-believers, concerning what this actually consists in The unifying characteristic of the qualities I have described as 'spiritual' may be said to be some level of concern for others' well-being. In Tibetan, we speak of *shen-pen kyi-sem* meaning, literally, 'the thought to be of help to others'. And when we consider them, we see that each of the qualities noted are defined by an implicit concern for others' well-being. Moreover, the one who is compassionate, loving, patient, tolerant, forgiving to some extent recognizes the potential impact of their actions on others. These individuals order their conduct accordingly. Therefore, spiritual practice entails, acting out of concern for the well-being of others. It also entails changing ourselves so that we become more readily disposed to do so. To speak of spiritual practice in any terms other than these is meaningless.

My call for a spiritual revolution is thus not a call for a religious revolution. Nor is it a reference to a way of life that is somehow other-worldly, still less to something magical or mysterious. Rather it is a call for a radical re-orientation away from our habitual preoccupation with self towards concern for the wider community of beings with whom we are connected, and for conduct which recognizes others' interests alongside our own.

Here the reader may object that the transformation of character that such a re-orientation implies is certainly desirable, and whilst it is good that people develop compassion and love: a revolution of spirit is hardly adequate to solve the variety and magnitude of problems we face in the modern world. Furthermore, it could be argued that our problems arising from, for example, violence in the home, addiction to drugs and alcohol, the break-up of the family and so on, are better understood and tackled on their own terms. Nevertheless, given that each could certainly be solved through people being more loving and compassionate towards one another – however improbable this may be – they can also be characterized as spiritual problems susceptible to a spiritual solution. This is not to say that all we need do is cultivate spiritual values and these problems will automatically disappear. On the contrary, each of them needs a specific solution. But we find that where this spiritual or inner dimension is neglected, we have no hope of achieving a lasting solution.

Why is this? Bad news is a fact of life. Each time we pick up a newspaper, or turn on the television or radio, we are confronted with sad tidings. Not a day goes by but, somewhere in the world, something happens which everyone agrees is unfortunate. No matter where we are from or what our philosophy of life, to a greater or lesser extent, we are all sorry to hear of others' suffering.

These events can be divided into two broad categories: those which have principally natural causes – earthquakes, drought, floods and the like – and those which are of human origin. Wars, crime, violence of every sort, corruption, poverty, nepotism, deception, fraud, social, political and economic injustice are each the consequence of negative human behaviour.

Fortunately, unlike natural disasters about which we can

do little or nothing, these human problems, because they are all essentially ethical problems, can be overcome. The fact that there are so many people, again from every sector and level of society, working to do so is a reflection of this intuition. There are those who join political parties to fight for a fairer constitution. There are those who become lawyers to fight for justice. There are those who join aid organizations to fight poverty. And there are those who care, both on a professional and on a voluntary basis, for the victims of harm. Indeed we are all, according to our own understanding and in our own way, trying to make the world – or at least our bit of it – a better place in which to live.

Unfortunately, we find that no matter how sophisticated and well-administered our legal systems, and no matter how advanced our methods of external control, they cannot eradicate wrongdoing by themselves. Observe that nowadays our police forces have at their disposal technology that could barely have been imagined fifty years ago. They have methods of surveillance which enable them to see what formerly was hidden; they have DNA matching, forensic laboratories, sniffer dogs and, of course, highly trained personnel. Yet criminal methods are correspondingly advanced so that really we are no better off.

Where ethical restraint is lacking, there can be no hope of overcoming problems like those of rising crime. In fact, without such inner discipline, we find that the very means we use to solve them becomes a source of difficulty. The increasing sophistication of criminal and police methods – a vicious and mutually reinforcing cycle – testifies to this.

What, then, is the relationship between spirituality and ethical practice? Observe that since love and compassion and all similar qualities, by definition, presume some level of concern for others' well-being, they must also presume ethical restraint. We cannot be loving and compassionate unless we curb our own harmful impulses and desires at the same time.

As to the foundations of ethical practice itself, it might be supposed that here at least I advocate a religious approach. Certainly each of the major religious traditions has a well-developed ethical system. However, the difficulty with tying our understanding of right and wrong to religion is that we must then ask 'which religion?' Which articulates the most complete, the most accessible, the most acceptable system? The arguments would never stop. Moreover, to do so would be to ignore the fact that many who reject religion do so out of convictions sincerely held, not merely because they are unconcerned with the deeper questions of human existence. We are not to suppose that such people are without a sense of right and wrong or of what is morally appropriate just because some who are anti-religion are immoral. Besides, religious belief is no guarantee of moral integrity. Looking at the history of our species, we see that among the major troublemakers – those who visited violence, brutality and destruction on their fellow human beings – there have been many who professed religious faith, often loudly. Religion can help us establish basic ethical principles. Yet we can still talk about ethics and morality without having recourse to religion.

Again, the objection could be made that if we do not accept religion as the source of ethics, we must allow that peoples' understanding of what is good and right, of what is wrong and bad, of what is morally appropriate and what is not, of what constitutes a positive act and what a negative act, must vary according to circumstances and even from person to person. Here let me say that no one should suppose it could ever be possible to devise a set of rules or laws to provide us with the answer to every ethical dilemma, even if we were to accept religion as the basis of morality. Such a formulaic approach could never hope to capture the richness and diversity of human experience. It would also include the possibility of arguing that we are responsible only to the letter of those laws, rather than for our actions.

This is not to say that it is useless to attempt to construe principles which can be understood as morally binding. On the contrary, if we are to have any hope of solving our problems, it is essential we find a way to do so. We must have some means of adjudicating between, for example, terrorism as a means to political reform and Mahatma Gandhi's principles of peaceful resistance. We must be able to show that violence towards others is wrong. And yet we must find some way of doing so which avoids the extremes of crude absolutism on the one hand, and of trivial relativism on the other.

My own view — which does not rely solely on religious faith, nor even on an original idea, but rather on ordinary common sense — is that establishing binding ethical principles is possible when we take as our starting point the observation that we all desire happiness and not to suffer. We have no means of discriminating between right and wrong if we do not take into account others' feelings, others' suffering. And if it is correct that this aspiration is a settled disposition shared by all, it follows that each individual has a right to pursue happiness and avoid suffering.

From this we can infer that one of the things which determines whether an act is ethical or not is its effect on another's, or others', experience or expectation of happiness. An act which harms or does violence to this is potentially an unethical act.

I say potentially because although the consequences of our actions are important, there are other factors to consider, including both the question of intent and the nature of the act itself. We can all think of things that we have done which have upset others though it was by no means our intention to do so. Similarly, it is not hard to think of acts which, though they may appear somewhat forceful and aggressive and likely to cause hurt could yet contribute to others' happiness in the long term. Disciplining children will often fall into this category. On the other hand, when our intentions are selfish, the fact that our actions may appear to be gentle does not mean that they are positive or ethical. On the contrary, if for example our intention is to mislead, then to pretend kindness is a most unfortunate deed. Though force may not be involved, such an act is certainly violent. It does violence not only insofar as the end is harmful to the other, but also in that it injures that person's trust – their expectation of truth.

Again, it is not difficult to imagine a case where an individual may suppose their actions to be well-intended and directed towards the greater good of others, but where they are in reality totally immoral. Here we might think of a soldier who carries out orders summarily to execute civilian prisoners. Believing the cause to be a just one, this soldier may suppose such actions to be directed towards the greater good of humanity. But if murder is unlawful killing then it is by definition an unethical act. Carrying out such orders would thus be gravely negative conduct. In other words, the content of our actions is also important in determining whether they are ethical or not, since certain acts are negative by definition.

The factor which is perhaps most important of all in determining the ethical nature of an act is neither its content, nor its consequence, however. In fact, the fruits of our actions are rarely directly attributable to us alone – whether the helmsman is able to bring his boat to safety in a storm depends not on his actions alone. In Tibetan, the term for that which is considered to be of the greatest significance in determining the ethical value of a given action is the individual's *kun-long*. Translated literally, the participle *kun* means 'thoroughly' or 'from the depths' and *'long(wa)'* denotes the act of causing something to stand up, to arise, or to awaken. But in the sense in which it used here, *kun-long* is understood as that which, in a sense, drives or inspires our actions – both those we intend directly and those which are in a sense involuntary. It therefore denotes the individual's overall state of heart and mind. When this is wholesome, it follows that our actions themselves will be ethically wholesome.

From this description, it is clear that it is difficult to translate *kun-long* succinctly. Generally, it is rendered simply as 'motivation'. Clearly, this does not capture the full range of its meaning. The word 'disposition', also comes quite close, but lacks the active sense of the Tibetan. On the other hand, to use the term overall state of heart and mind seems unnecessarily clumsy. Arguably, it could be abbreviated to mind-state, but this would be to ignore the wider meaning of mind as it is used in Tibetan. The word for mind, *lo*, includes the ideas of consciousness, or awareness, alongside those of feeling and emotion. This reflects an understanding that emotions and thoughts cannot finally be separated. Thus even the perception of a quality, like colour, is held to carry within it an affective dimension, a 'tonal' quality. Nor is there an idea of pure sensation without any accompanying cognitive event. The understanding is rather that we can identify different types of emotion. There are those which are primarily instinctual, such as revulsion at the sight of blood, and there are those which have a more developed rational component such as fear of poverty. The reader is asked to remember this point whenever I speak of mind, of motivation, of disposition, or of states of mind.

That this is so, that the individual's overall state of heart and mind, or motivation, in the moment of action is of supreme importance in determining its ethical content, is easily understood when we consider how our actions are affected when we are gripped with powerful negative thoughts and emotions such as hatred and anger. In that moment, our mind (lo) is in turmoil. Not only does this cause us to lose our sense of proportion and perspective, it also causes us to lose sight of the likely impact of our actions on others. Indeed, we can become so distracted that we ignore the question of others, and of their right to happiness altogether. As a result, our actions – that is to say our deeds, words, thoughts, omissions and desires – will inevitably be harmful. And this is in spite of what our long term intentions towards others may be or whether our actions are consciously intended or not. Consider a situation in which we become embroiled in an argument with a family member. How we deal with the charged atmosphere which develops will depend to a large extent on what underlies our actions at that moment – in other words, our *kun-long*. The less calm we are, the more likely we are to react negatively with harsh words even though we feel deeply for that person and the more certain we are to say or do things which later we regret bitterly.

Or imagine a situation where we inconvenience another in some small way, perhaps by bumping into them accidently whilst walking along. They shout at us for being careless. We are much more likely to shrug this off if our disposition (*kun-long*) is wholesome, if our hearts are suffused with compassion, than if we are under the sway of negative emotions. When the driving force of our actions is wholesome, our actions will tend automatically to contribute to others' well-being. They will thus automatically be ethical. Further, the more this is our habitual state, the less likely we are to react badly when provoked. And even when we do lose our temper, any outburst will be free of any sense of malice or hatred. The aim of spiritual and, in the widest sense, ethical practice is thus to transform and perfect the individual's *kun-long* – to make us better human beings, in other words.

We find that the more we succeed in transforming our hearts and minds through cultivating spiritual qualities, the better able we will be to cope with adversity and the greater the likelihood that our actions will be ethically wholesome. So if I may be permitted to give my own case as an example, this understanding of ethics means that I strive continuously to cultivate a positive, or wholesome

ANCIENT WISDOM, MODERN WORLD

overall state of heart and mind. At the same time, I try to be of the greatest service to others that I can be. By making sure, on top of this, that the content of my actions is, so far as I am able to make them, similarly positive, I reduce my chances of acting unethically. How effective this strategy is, that is to say, what the consequences are in terms of others' well-being, either in the short-term or the long-term, there is no way to tell. But provided my efforts are continuous, and provided I pay attention, no matter what happens, I should never have cause for regret. And at least I know I have done my best.

My description in this chapter of the relationship between ethics and spirituality does not address the question of how we are to resolve ethical dilemmas. We will come to that later. Rather I have been concerned to outline an approach to ethics which, by relating ethical discourse to the basic human experience of happiness and suffering, avoids the problems which arise when we ground ethics in religion. The reality is that the majority of people today are unpersuaded of the need for religion. Moreover, there may be conduct which is acceptable to one religious tradition but not to another. As to what I mean by the term spiritual revolution, I trust that I have made clear that a spiritual revolution entails an ethical revolution.

CHAPTER THREE

DEPENDENT ORIGINATION AND THE NATURE OF REALITY

At a public talk I gave in Japan some years ago, I saw some people coming towards me carrying a bunch of flowers. I stood up in anticipation of receiving their offering, but to my surprise, they walked straight past and laid the flowers on the altar behind. I sat down feeling somewhat embarrassed! Yet again I was reminded that the way in which things and events unfold does not always coincide with our expectations. Indeed, this fact of life – that there is often a gap between the way in which we perceive phenomena and the reality of a given situation –

ANCIENT WISDOM, MODERN WORLD

is the source of much unhappiness. This is especially true
when, as in the example here, we make judgements on the
basis of a partial understanding which turns out not to be
fully justified.

Before considering what a spiritual and ethical revolution might consist in, let us give some thought to the
nature of reality itself. The close connection between
how we perceive ourselves in relation to the world we
inhabit and our behaviour in response to it means that
our understanding of phenomena is crucially significant.

In the course of our daily lives, we engage in countless
different activities and receive huge sensory input from
all that we encounter. The problem of misconception,
which of course varies in degree, usually arises because of
our tendency to isolate particular aspects of an event or
experience and see them as constituting its totality. This
leads to a narrowing of perspective and from there to
false expectations. If we consider reality itself, we quickly
become aware of its infinite complexity. Our habitual
perception of it is therefore inadequate. If this were not so,
the concept of deception would be meaningless. If things
and events always unfolded as we expected them to, we
would have no notion of illusion or misconception.

As a means to understanding this complexity, I find
the concept of dependent origination (in Tibetan, *ten del*),
articulated by the Madhyamika (Middle Way) school of
Buddhist philosophy to be particularly helpful. According
to this, we can understand how things and events come

to be in three different ways. At the first level, the principle of cause and effect is invoked whereby all things and events arise in dependence on a complex web of interrelated causes and conditions. From this, we see that no thing or event can be construed as capable of existing in and of itself. For example, if I take some clay and mould it, I can bring a pot into being. The pot exists as an effect of my actions. At the same time, it is also the effect of a myriad of other causes and conditions. These include the combination of clay and water to form its raw material. Beyond this we can point to the coming together of the molecules, the atoms and other minute particles which form these constituents – which are themselves dependent on innumerable other factors. Then there are the circumstances leading up to my decision to make a pot, and there are the cooperative conditions of my actions as I give shape to the clay. All these different factors make it clear that my pot cannot exist independently of its causes and conditions. Rather it is dependently originated.

On another level, *ten-del* can be understood in terms of the mutual dependence which exists between parts and whole. Without parts there can be no whole; without a whole the concept of parts makes no sense. This is not to deny that, in a sense, the idea of 'whole' is predicated on parts. Thus parts do enjoy a comparatively more substantial or identifiable reality. But then these parts themselves must be considered to be wholes comprised of their own parts.

On the third level, all things and events can be understood to be dependently originated on account of the fact that when we analyse them, we find that, ultimately, they lack independent identity. This is seen at a gross level from the way in which we refer to certain phenomena. For example, the words 'action' and 'agent' presuppose each other. So do 'parent' and 'child'. Someone is only a parent because he or she has children. Likewise, a daughter or son is so called only in relation to their parents. The same relationship of mutual dependence is seen in the language we use to describe trades or professions. Individuals are called farmers on account of their work on the land. Doctors are so called in dependence on their work in the field of medicine.

In a more subtle way, things and events are seen to be dependently originated when, for example, we ask what exactly is a clay pot? When we look for something we can describe as its essence, we find that the pot's very existence – and by implication that of all other phenomena – is to some extent provisional and determined by convention. When we ask whether its identity is determined by its shape, its function, its specific parts (that is, its being compounded of clay and water), we find that the term 'pot' is merely a verbal designation. There is no single characteristic which can be said to identify it. Nor indeed does the totality of its characteristics. We can imagine pots of different shapes that are no less pots. And because its identity can only be established in relation to a complex nexus of causes and conditions, it is better described as being in some sense emergent, or contingent. In other words, things and events do not exist in and of themselves but rather they are dependently originated.

Insofar as non-physical phenomena are concerned we see that again there is a dependence. Here it lies between perceiver and perceived. Take, for example, the perception of a flower. First, in order for the perception of a flower to arise, there must be a sense organ. Second, there must be a condition – in this case the flower itself. Third, there must be something which directs the focus of the perceiver to the object. Then, through the causal interaction of these conditions, a cognitive event occurs which we call the perception of a flower. Now let us examine what exactly constitutes this event? Is it the operation of the sense faculty? Is it the interaction between that faculty and the flower itself? Or is it something else? We find that in the end, we are left with an event which takes place which we call 'perception'. We cannot understand the concept of perception except in the context of an infinitely complex series of causes and conditions. Furthermore, if we take consciousness itself as the object of our investigation, although we tend to think of it in terms of a monolithic entity, we find that it, too, is better understood in terms of dependent origination. This is because apart from individual perceptual, cognitive and emotional experiences, it is difficult to posit an independently existing entity. Rather, consciousness is more like a construct that arises out of a spectrum of complex events that are also dependently originated.

Another way to understand the concept of dependent origination is to consider the phenomenon of time. Ordinarily, we suppose that there is an independently existing entity which we call time. We speak of time past, present, and future. However, when we look more closely, we again see that this concept is merely a convention. We find that the term 'present moment' is just a label denoting the interface between the tenses 'past' and 'future'. We cannot actually pinpoint the present. Just a fraction of a second before the supposed present moment lies the past; just a fraction of a second after lies the future. Yet if we say that the present moment is 'now', no sooner have we spoken the word than it lies in the past. If we were to maintain that there must be a single moment which is indivisible into either past or future, we would in fact have no grounds for any separation into past, present and future at all. If there is a single moment which is indivisible, then we would have only the present. Yet if the present cannot be posited, it becomes difficult to speak about the past and the future since clearly both depend on the present. Moreover, if we were to conclude from our analysis that the present does not then exist, we would have to deny not only worldly convention but also our own experience. Indeed, when we begin to analyse our experience of time, we find that here the past disappears and the future is yet to come. We experience only the present.

Where do these observations leave us? Certainly things become somewhat more complex when we think along these lines. The more satisfactory conclusion is surely to say that the present does indeed exist. But it does not do so inherently or objectively. It exists in dependence on the past and the future.

Such an understanding of reality as that suggested by this concept of dependent origination presents us with a significant challenge. It challenges us to see it less in terms of black and white and more in terms of a complex interlinking of relationships which are hard to pin down. Small wonder if we are often mistaken in our understanding of what is real and what we suppose to be real. For if all phenomena are dependent on other phenomena and if no phenomena can exist independently, even our most cherished selves must be considered not to exist in the way we normally assume. Indeed, we find that if we search for the identity of the self analytically, even more readily than the clay pot or the present moment, its apparent solidity dissolves. Whereas a pot is something concrete to which we can actually point, the self is more elusive: its identity as a construct quickly becomes evident.

This is not to deny that every human being naturally and correctly has a strong sense of 'I'. Even though we might not be able to say why it is so, this sense of self is certainly there. But let us examine what constitutes the

ANCIENT WISDOM, MODERN WORLD

actual object we call self. Is it the mind? Sometimes it happens that an individual's mind becomes hyperactive, or it may become depressed. In either case, a doctor may prescribe medicine in order to improve that person's sense of well-being. This shows that we think of the mind as, in a sense, a possession of the self. Indeed when we think closely, statements such as 'my body', 'my speech', 'my mind' all have within them an implied notion of ownership. It is difficult, therefore, to see how mind can constitute self, although it is true that there have been Buddhist philosophers who tried to identify self with consciousness. If this were correct, it would follow that the actor and the action, both the doer and what is done are one and the same. We would have to say that the agent 'I' who knows and the process of knowing are identical. The statement 'I know' would thus be meaningless. If, on the other hand, the self exists as an independent phenomenon, it must do so outside the mind-body aggregate. This is equally untenable. We must therefore conclude, that our notion of self is a label for a complex web of interrelated phenomena.

Here let us step back and review how we normally relate to this idea of self. We say, 'I am tall. I am short. I did this. I did that.' And nobody questions us. It is quite clear what we mean and everybody is happy to accept the convention. On this level, we exist quite in accordance with these statements. Such convention is part of everyday discourse and is compatible with common experience. But this does not mean that something exists solely because it is said to exist. Conventions may be said to be valid when they do not contradict knowledge acquired either through empirical experience or through inference. On this basis, they serve as the foundation for a common discourse within which we situate such notions as truth and falsity. This does not preclude us from accepting that, although perfectly adequate as a convention, the self, as with all other phenomena, exists in dependence on the labels and concepts we apply to the term. Consider in this context an instance in which we mistake a coiled rope for a snake in the dark. We stop still and feel afraid. Although what we see is in reality a length of rope that we may have forgotten, because of the lack of light and due to our misconception, we think it is a snake. Actually, the coil of rope possesses not the slightest quality of a snake except in appearances. We have imputed its existence onto an inanimate object. The snake itself is not there. So it is with the notion of an independently existing self.

We also find that the very concept of self is relative. Here consider the fact that we often find ourselves in situations in which we blame ourselves. We say 'Oh on such and such a day I really let myself down.' We speak of feeling angry with ourselves. This suggests that there are in fact two distinct selves, the one who did something wrong and the one who criticizes. The former is a self understood in relation to a particular experience or event.

The latter is understood from a perspective of the self as a generality. Yet even though it makes sense to have an internal dialogue, still there is only one continuum of self. Similarly, we can see that the personal identity of a single individual has many different aspects. In my own case, for example, there is a self that is a monk, a self that is Tibetan, a self that is from the Amdo region of Tibet, and so on. Some of these selves pre-date others. For instance, the self which is Tibetan existed before the self that is a monk. I did not become a novice monk until I was seven years old. The self which is a refugee has only existed since 1959. In other words, on one single basis there are many designations. They are all Tibetan since that self – or identity – existed at my birth. But they are all nominally different. We cannot therefore say that any one characteristic is what finally constitutes my 'self'. Nor, on the other hand, is it the sum of them. For even if I were to relinquish one or more, the sense of 'I' would remain.

Thus there is no single thing that can be found under analysis to identify the self. We find that just as when we try to find the ultimate identity of a solid object, it eludes us. Indeed, we are forced to conclude that this precious thing of which we take such care, and which we go to such lengths to protect and make comfortable is, in the end, no more substantial than a rainbow in the summer sky.

If this is true, that no object or phenomena, not even the

self, exists inherently, should we then conclude that, ultimately, nothing exists at all? Or is the reality we perceive simply a projection of the mind, apart from which nothing exists? No. When we say that things and events can only be established in terms of their dependently originating nature, that they are without intrinsic reality, existence or identity, we are not denying the existence of phenomena altogether. The 'identitylessness' of phenomena points rather to the way in which things exist: not independently but, in a sense, *inter*dependently. Far from undermining the notion of phenomenal reality, the concept of dependent origination provides a robust framework within which to situate cause and effect, truth and falsity, identity and difference, harm and benefit. It is therefore quite wrong to infer from the idea any sort of nihilistic approach to reality. A simple nothingness, without any sense of an object being this and not that is absolutely not my meaning. Indeed if we take 'lack of identity' as the object of further enquiry and search for its true nature, what we find is the identitylessness of identitylessness and so on, going into infinity – from which we must conclude that even the absence of intrinsic existence exists only conventionally.

One of the most promising developments in modern science is the emergence of quantum theory. To some degree at least, this appears to support the notion of the independent origination of phenomena. I cannot claim to have a very clear understanding of quantum theory, but the observation that, at the subatomic level, it becomes difficult to distinguish clearly between the observer of an object and the object itself, seems to indicate a movement towards the conception of reality I have outlined. I would not wish to emphasize this too strongly, however. What science holds to be true today is liable to change. New discoveries mean that what is accepted today may be doubted tomorrow. Besides, on whatever premise we base our appreciation of the fact that things and events do not exist independently, the consequences are similar. We find that we cannot finally separate out any phenomena from the context of other phenomena. We can only really speak in terms of relationships.

How does this help us? What is the value of these observations? They have a number of important implications. Firstly, when we come to see that everything we perceive and experience arises as a result of an infinity of dependently originated and interrelated causes and conditions, our whole perspective changes. We begin to see that the universe we inhabit can be understood in terms of a living organism in which each cell works in balanced cooperation with every other cell to sustain the whole. If just one of these cells is harmed, as it is when disease strikes, that balance is harmed and there is danger to the whole. This in turn suggests that our individual well-being is intimately connected both with that of all others and with the environment within which we live. It also becomes apparent that our every action, our every deed, word and thought, no matter how slight or inconsequential it may seem, has an implication not only for ourselves but for all others too.

Furthermore, when we view reality in terms of dependent origination, it draws us away from our usual tendency to see things and events in terms of solid, independent, discrete entities. This is helpful in that it is this tendency which causes us to exaggerate one or two aspects of our experience and make them representative of the whole reality of a given situation whilst ignoring its wider complexities. Most importantly, we come to see that the habitual sharp distinction we make between 'self' and 'others' is itself an exaggeration.

Such an understanding of reality also allows us to see that this sharp distinction between self and others arises largely as a result of conditioning. And it is possible to imagine becoming habituated to an extended conception of self wherein the individual situates his or her interests within the interests of others. For example, when an individual thinks in terms of his or her homeland, and says 'We are Tibetan' or 'We are French' they understand their identity in terms of something that goes beyond that of the individual self.

If the self had intrinsic identity, it would be possible to speak in terms of self-interest in isolation from that of others. But given that this is not so, given that self and others can only be understood in terms of relationship, we see that self-interest and the interests of others are similarly interrelated. Indeed, within this picture of dependently originated reality, we see that there is no self-interest completely unrelated to others' interests. Due to the fundamental interconnectedness which lies at the heart of reality, your interest is also my interest. Thus my happiness is to a large extent dependent on yours. From this, it becomes clear that 'my' interests and 'your' interests are intimately connected. In a deep sense, they converge. Because of this, if we wish for our own happiness, we have to consider others. It is a practical necessity that we do so.

One other important consequence of the concept of reality discussed in this chapter is that it becomes very difficult to speak in terms of absolutes. However, while acknowledging that there is often a discrepancy between perception and reality, it is important not to go to the extreme of assuming that behind the phenomenal is a realm which is somehow more 'real'. The problem with this is that we may then dismiss everyday experience as nothing but an illusion. This would be quite wrong. Similarly, accepting a more complex understanding of reality, in which all things and events are seen to be interdependent, does not mean we cannot infer that the ethical principles we identified earlier cannot be understood as binding. On the contrary, the concept of dependent origination compels us to take the reality of cause and effect with utmost seriousness. By this I mean the fact that particular causes lead to particular effects, that certain actions lead to suffering while others lead to happiness. Thus it is in everybody's interest to seek those that lead to happiness and avoid those which lead to suffering. And because, as we have seen, our interests are inextricably linked, we are compelled to accept ethics as the indispensable interface between my desire to be happy and yours.

CHAPTER FOUR

REDEFINING THE GOAL

I have observed that we all naturally desire happiness and to avoid suffering. I have suggested, furthermore, this is a right from which we can infer that an ethical act is one which does not harm another's experience or expectation of happiness. I have also described an understanding of reality which points to a commonality of interest in respect of self and others.

Let us now consider the nature of happiness. The first thing to note is that happiness is a relative quality. We experience it differently according to our circumstances. What makes one person glad may be a source of suffering to another. Most of us would be extremely sorry to be sent to prison for life. Yet a criminal under threat of the death penalty would likely be very happy to be reprieved with a sentence of life imprisonment. Secondly, it is important to recognize that we use the same word 'happiness' to describe very different states, although this is more obvious in Tibetan where the same word *de-wa* is used for 'pleasure' also. We speak of happiness in connection with bathing in cool water on a hot day. We speak of it in connection with certain ideal states such as when we say I would be so happy to win the lottery. We also speak of happiness in relation to the simple joys of family life.

In this last example, happiness is more a state which persists in spite of ups and downs and occasional intermissions. But in the case of bathing in cool water on a hot day, because it is the consequence of activities which seek to please the senses, it is necessarily transient. If we remain in the water too long, we start to feel cold. Indeed, the happiness we derive from such activities depends on them being short-lived. So far as the case of winning a large sum of money is concerned, the question of whether it would confer lasting happiness or merely the sort that is soon overwhelmed by problems and difficulties that cannot be solved by wealth alone depends upon the individual who wins it. But generally speaking, even if money brings us happiness, it tends to be the kind which money can buy: material things and sensory experiences. And these, we discover, become a source of suffering themselves. As far as actual possessions are concerned we must admit that they often cause us more, not less difficulties in life. The car breaks down, we lose our money, our most precious belongings are stolen, our house is damaged by fire. Or, we worry about these things happening.

If such actions and circumstances did not contain within them the seeds of suffering, the more we indulged in them, the greater our happiness would be – just as pain increases the more we endure the causes of pain. In fact, whilst occasionally we may feel we have found perfect happiness of this sort, this seeming perfection turns out to be as ephemeral as a drop of dew on a leaf, shining brilliantly one moment, gone the next.

This explains why placing too much hope in material development is mistaken. The problem is not materialism as such. Rather it is the underlying assumption that full satisfaction can arise from gratifying the senses alone. Unlike animals whose quest for happiness is restricted to survival and to the immediate gratification of sensory desires, we human beings have the capacity to experience happiness at a deeper level which, when achieved, can overwhelm unhappy experiences. Here consider a soldier who fights in a battle. He is wounded, but the battle is won. The satisfaction he experiences in victory means that his experience of suffering on account of his wounds will likely be far less than those of a soldier with the same wounds on the losing side.

This human capacity for experiencing deeper levels of

happiness also explains why such things as music and the arts offer a greater degree of happiness and satisfaction than merely acquiring material objects. However, even though aesthetic experiences are a source of happiness, they also have a strong sensory component. Music depends on the ears, art on the eyes, dance on the body. As with the satisfactions we derive from work or career, they are in general acquired through the senses. By themselves, they cannot offer the happiness we dream of.

Now, it could be argued that whilst it is all very well to distinguish happiness that is transient from that which is lasting, between ephemeral and genuine happiness, the only happiness it is meaningful to speak of when a person is dying from thirst is access to water. This is unarguable. When it comes to the question of survival, naturally our needs become so urgent that the majority of our efforts will go towards fulfilling them. Yet because the urge to survive comes out of physical need, it follows that bodily satisfaction is invariably limited to what the senses provide. To conclude that we should seek immediate gratification in all circumstances would hardly be justified. Actually, when we think carefully, we see that the brief elation we experience appeasing sensual impulses is very close to what the drug addict feels when indulging his or her habit. Temporary relief is soon followed by a craving for more. And in just the same way that taking drugs in the end only causes trouble, so too does much of what we undertake to fulfil our immediate sensory desires. This is not to say that the pleasure we take in certain activities is somehow mistaken. But we must acknowledge that there can be no hope of gratifying the senses permanently. At best, the happiness we derive from eating a good meal can only last until the next time we are hungry. As an ancient Indian writer remarked:

Indulging our senses and drinking salt water are alike: the more we partake, the more our desire and thirst grow.

Indeed, we find that a great deal of what I have called internal suffering can be attributed to our impulsive approach to happiness. We do not stop to consider the complexity of a given situation. Our tendency is to rush in and do that which seems to promise the shortest route to satisfaction. In doing so, all too frequently we deprive ourselves of the opportunity of a greater degree of fulfilment. This is actually quite strange. Usually we do not allow our children to do whatever they want. We realize that, given their freedom, it is likely they would spend their time playing rather than studying. Instead we make them sacrifice the immediate pleasure of play and compel them to study. Our strategy is more long term. While this may be less fun for them, it confers a solid foundation for their future. But as adults we often neglect this principle. We overlook the fact that if, for example, one partner in a marriage devotes all their time to their own narrow interests, the other partner will suffer.

If this happens, it is inevitable the marriage will become harder and harder to sustain. Similarly, there are sure to be negative consequences for the parents who are interested only in each other and who neglect their children.

The fact is, when we act to fulfil our immediate desires without taking into account others' interests, we undermine the possibility of any sort of lasting happiness. Consider that if we live in a neighbourhood with ten other families and yet we never give a thought to their well-being, we rob ourselves of the opportunity to benefit from their society. On the other hand, if we make the effort to be friendly and have regard for their well-being, we provide for our own happiness as well as theirs. Or again, imagine an instance where we meet somebody new. Perhaps we go for a meal together. Now this may cost us some money. But as a result, there is a good chance of founding a relationship which brings many benefits over the years to come. Conversely, if on meeting someone we see a chance to defraud them, and we take it, though we have gained a sum of money instantly, the likelihood is that we completely destroy the possibility of a long term benefit from interaction with them.

Now let us consider the nature of what I have characterized as genuine happiness. Here my own experience might serve to illustrate the state I am describing. As a Buddhist monk, I have been trained in the practice, the philosophy and the principles of Buddhism. But as to any sort of education to cope with the demands of modern living, I have received almost none. During the course of my life, I have had to handle enormous responsibilities and difficulties. At sixteen, I lost my freedom when Tibet was occupied. At twenty-four, I lost my country itself when I came into exile. For forty years now, I have lived as a refugee in a foreign country, albeit the one that it is my spiritual home. Throughout this time, I have been trying to serve my fellow refugees and, to the extent possible, the Tibetans who remain in Tibet. Meanwhile our homeland has known immeasurable destruction and suffering. And of course I have lost not only my mother and other close family members but also dear friends. Yet for all this, although I certainly feel sad when I think about these losses, still so far as my basic serenity is concerned, on most days I am calm and contented. Even when difficulties arise, as they must, I am usually not much bothered by them. I have no hesitation in saying that I am happy.

According to my experience, then, the principle characteristic of genuine happiness is peace: inner peace. By this I do not mean some kind of feeling of being 'spaced out'. Nor am I speaking of an absence of feeling. On the contrary, the peace I am describing is rooted in concern for others and involves a high degree of sensitivity and feeling, although I cannot claim personally to have succeeded very far in this. Rather, I attribute my sense of peace to the effort to develop concern for others.

This fact, that inner peace is the principle characteristic of happiness explains the paradox that, whilst we can all think of people who remain dissatisfied, despite having every material advantage, there are others who remain happy, notwithstanding the most difficult circumstances. Consider the example of those eighty thousand Tibetans who, during the months following my escape into exile, left Tibet for the sanctuary offered them by the Indian government. The conditions they faced were hard in the extreme. There was little food available and even less medicine. The refugee camps could offer no better accommodation than canvas tents. Most people had few possessions beyond the clothes they wore: heavy *chubas* (the traditional Tibetan dress) appropriate to our harsh winters. What they really needed in India was the lightest cotton. And there was terrible sickness from diseases unknown in Tibet. Yet for all their hardship, today, the survivors exhibit few signs of trauma. Even then, few entirely lost confidence. Fewer still gave into their feelings of sorrow and despair. I would even say that, once the initial shock had passed, the majority remained quite optimistic and, yes, happy.

The indication here is that, if we can develop this quality of inner peace, no matter what difficulties we meet with in life, our basic sense of well-being will not be undermined. It also follows that, though there is no denying the importance of external factors in bringing this about, we are mistaken if we suppose that they can ever make us completely happy.

Certainly our constitution, our upbringing, our circumstances all contribute to our experience of happiness. And we can all agree that the lack of certain things make the attainment of happiness all the harder. So let us consider these in turn. Good health, friends, freedom, a degree of prosperity all of these are valuable and helpful. Good health speaks for itself. We all desire it. Similarly, we all need and want friends, no matter what our situation or how successful we become. (I have always been fascinated by watches and though I am particularly fond of the one I generally wear, it never shows me any affection!) In order to attain the satisfactions of love, we need friends who can return our affection. Of course there are different kinds of friends. There are those who are really the friends of status, money and fame, and not the friends of the person who possesses these things. But I refer to those who are there to help us when we encounter a difficult stage in life and not those who base their relationship with us on superficial attributes.

Freedom, in the sense of liberty to pursue happiness and to hold and express personal views likewise contributes to our sense of inner peace. In societies in which this is not permitted, we find spies who pry into the lives of every community, even the family itself. The inevitable result is that people start to lose confidence in one another. They become suspicious and doubt each other's motives. Once a person's basic sense of trust is destroyed, how can we expect them to be happy?

Prosperity – not so much in the sense of having an abundance of material wealth but more in the sense of flourishing mentally and emotionally – also makes a significant contribution to our sense of inner peace. Here again, we might think of the example of the Tibetan refugees who prospered in spite of their lack of resources. Indeed, each of these factors plays an important part in establishing a sense of individual well-being. Yet without a basic feeling of inner peace and security, they are of no avail. Why? Because our possessions themselves can be a source of anxiety. So can our jobs insofar as we worry about losing them. Even our friends and relatives may become a source of trouble. They may get sick and need our attention when we are busy with important business. They may even turn against us and cheat us. Similarly, our bodies, however fit and beautiful they may be at present, must eventually give in to old age. Nor are we ever invulnerable to sickness and pain. Thus there is no hope of attaining lasting happiness if we lack inner peace.

Where then are we to find inner peace? There is no single answer. But one thing is for sure. No external factor can create it. Nor would it be any use asking for inner peace from a doctor. The best he or she could do is offer us an antidepressant, or a sleeping pill. Similarly, no machine or computer, however sophisticated and powerful, could give us this vital quality. Instead, we find that developing inner peace, on which lasting –

and therefore meaningful – happiness is dependent, is like any other task in life. We have to identify its causes and conditions and then diligently set about acquiring them. This, we find, entails a two-pronged approach. On the one hand, we need to guard against those factors which obstruct it. On the other, we need to cultivate those which are conducive to it.

So far as the conditions of inner peace are concerned, one of the most important is our basic attitude. Let me explain what I mean by this by giving another personal example. Despite my habitual serenity today, I used to be somewhat hot-tempered and prone to fits of impatience and sometimes anger. Even now, there are of course times when I lose my composure. When this happens, the least annoyance can take on undue proportions and upset me considerably. I may, for example, wake up in the morning and feel agitated for no particular reason. In this state, I find that even what ordinarily pleases me may irritate me. Just looking at my watch can give rise to feelings of annoyance. I see it as nothing but a source of attachment and, through this, of further suffering. But then on other days I will wake up and see it as something beautiful, so intricate and delicate. Yet of course it is the same watch. What has changed? Are my feelings of revulsion one day and satisfaction the next purely the result of chance? Or is some neurological mechanism over which I have no control at work here? No. Although biochemistry may have something to do with it, the governing factor is my mental attitude. Our basic outlook, how we relate to external circumstances is thus the first consideration in any discussion on developing inner peace. In this context, the great Indian scholar-practitioner Shantideva once observed that whilst we have no hope of finding enough leather to cover the earth so that we never prick our feet on a thorn, we actually do not need this much. He observed that enough leather to cover the soles of our feet will suffice. In other words, whilst we cannot always change our external situation to suit us, we can change our attitude.

The other major source of inner peace, and thus of genuine happiness, is of course the actions we undertake in our pursuit of happiness. These we can classify in terms of those which make a positive contribution towards it, those which have a neutral effect, and those which have a negative effect. By considering what differentiates the acts which make for lasting happiness from those which offer only a transient sense of well-being, we see that, in the latter case, the activities themselves have no positive value. We have a desire for something sweet perhaps, or for some fashionable item of clothing, or to experience something new. We have no real need of it, however, we simply want that thing or to enjoy that experience or sensation. We set about satisfying our craving without much thought. Now I am not suggesting there is necessarily anything wrong in this. An appetite for the concrete is part of human nature: we want to see, we want to touch, we want to possess. But, as I suggested earlier, it is essential we recognize that when we desire things for no real reason beyond the enjoyment they give us, ultimately they tend to bring us more problems. Moreover, we find that like the happiness which comes with gratifying such perceived needs, they are themselves in fact transient.

We must also acknowledge that it is this very lack of concern for consequences that underlies extreme actions, like inflicting pain on others, and even killing, itself – either of which could conceivably give some sort of pleasure for a short time. Or again, in the field of economic activity, the pursuit of profit without consideration of potentially negative consequences may give rise to feelings of great joy when success comes. But in the end there is suffering: the environment is polluted, our unscrupulous methods drive others out of business, the bombs we manufacture cause death and injury.

As to those activities which can lead to a sense of peace and lasting happiness, consider what happens when we do something we consider to be worthwhile. Perhaps we conceive a plan to cultivate some bare land and, eventually, after much effort, bring it to fruition. When we analyse activities of this sort, we find they involve discernment. They entail weighing up different factors, including both the likely and the possible consequences for ourselves and for others. In this process of evaluation, the question of morality, of whether our intended actions are ethical, arises automatically.

So whilst the initial impulse might be to be deceitful in order to attain some end, we reason that whilst we may gain temporary happiness this way, actually the long term consequences of behaving thus are likely to bring trouble. We therefore deliberately renounce one course of action in favour of another. And it is through achieving our aim by means of effort and self-sacrifice, through considering both the short benefit to us and the long term effects on others' happiness, and sacrificing the former for the latter, that we attain the happiness which is characterized by peace and by genuine satisfaction. Our differing responses to hardship confirm this. When we go on holiday, our basic motive is leisure. If, then, due to bad weather, due to clouds and rain, we are frustrated in our desire to spend time relaxing outside, our happiness is easily destroyed. On the other hand, when we seek not merely temporary satisfaction, but strive to achieve a goal – hunger, fatigue, discomfort – all count for nothing.

In other words, altruism is an essential component of those actions which lead to genuine happiness. There is thus an important distinction to be made between what we might call ethical acts and spiritual conduct. An ethical act is one which does not cause harm to others' experience or expectation of happiness. Spiritual conduct we can describe in terms of those qualities mentioned earlier of love, compassion, patience, forgiveness, humility, tolerance and so on which presume some level of concern for others' well-being. We find that those actions we undertake which are motivated not by narrow self-interest but out of our concern for others actually benefit ourselves. And not only that but they make our lives meaningful. At least this is my experience. Looking back over my life, I can say with full confidence that such things as the office of Dalai Lama, the political power it confers, even the comparative wealth it puts at my disposal, contribute not even a fraction to my feelings of happiness compared with the extent to which I have been able to benefit others, little though this may be.

Does this proposition stand up to analysis? Is conduct driven by the wish to help others the most effective way to bringing about genuine happiness? Consider the following. We humans are social beings. We come into the world as the result of others' actions. We survive here in dependence on others. Whether we like it or not, there is hardly a moment of our lives in which we do not benefit from others' activities. For this reason it is hardly surprising that most of our happiness arises in the context of our relationships with others. Nor is it so remarkable that our greatest joy should come when we are motivated by concern for others. But that is not all. We find that not only do altruistic actions bring about happiness but they also lessen our experience of suffering. Here I am not suggesting that the individual whose actions are motivated by the wish to bring others happiness necessarily meets with less misfortune than the one who does not. Sickness, old age, mishaps of one sort or another are the same for us all. But the sufferings which undermine our internal peace – anxiety, doubt, disappointment – these are definitely less.

What does this tell us? Firstly, because our every action has a universal dimension, a potential impact on others' happiness, ethics are necessary as a means to ensure that we do not harm one another. Secondly, it tells us that genuine happiness consists in those spiritual qualities of love and compassion, patience, tolerance and forgiveness and so on. For it is these which provide happiness for ourselves and others.

CHAPTER FIVE

NYING-JE, THE SUPREME EMOTION

On a recent trip to Europe, I took the opportunity to visit the site of the Nazi death camp at Auschwitz. Even though I had heard and read a great deal about the place, I found myself completely unprepared for the experience. My initial reaction to the sight of the ovens in which hundreds of thousands of my fellow human beings were burned was one of total revulsion. I was dumbfounded at the sheer calculation and detachment from feeling to which they bore horrifying testimony. Then, in the museum which forms part of the visitor centre, I saw a collection of shoes. A lot of them were patched or small, having obviously belonged to children and poor people. This saddened me particularly. What wrong could *they* possibly have done, what harm? I stopped and prayed – moved profoundly both for the victims and for the perpetrators of this calamity – that such a thing would never happen again. And, in the knowledge that, just as we all have the capacity to act selflessly out of concern for others' well-being, so do we all have the potential to be murderers and torturers, I vowed never to contribute in any way to such an enterprise.

Events such as those which occurred at Auschwitz are violent reminders of what can happen when individuals – and by extension, whole societies – lose touch with basic human feeling. This is why, although it is necessary to have legislation and international conventions in place as safeguards against future disasters of this kind, actually their deterrent value is not great. Much more effective and important than such legislation is our regard for one another's feelings at a simple human level.

When I speak of basic human feeling, I am not just thinking of something fleeting and vague, however. I refer to the capacity we all have to empathize with one another and which, in Tibetan we call *shen dug-ngal-wa-la mi-sö-pa*. Translated literally, this means 'the inability to bear the sight of another's suffering'. Given that this is what enables us to enter into, and to some extent participate in others' pain, it is one of our most significant characteristics. It is what causes us to start at the sound of a cry for help, to recoil at the sight of harm done to another, to suffer when confronted with others' suffering. And it is that which compels us to shut our eyes when we want to ignore others' distress.

Here, imagine walking along a road, deserted save for an elderly person just ahead of you. Suddenly, that person trips and falls. What do you do? I have no doubt that the majority of readers would go over to see whether they might help. Not all, perhaps. But even in the case of those who did not, there will at least be the same feeling, however faint, of concern which would motivate the majority to offer their assistance. In admitting that not everyone would go to the assistance of another in distress, I do not mean to suggest that in those few exceptions this capacity for empathy, which I have suggested to be universal, is entirely absent. It is certainly possible to imagine people who, after enduring years of warfare, are no longer moved at the sight of another's suffering. The same could be true of those who live in places where there is an atmosphere of violence and indifference to others. It is even possible to imagine a few who would exult at the sight of another's suffering. This does not prove that the capacity for empathy is not present in such people. That we all, excepting perhaps only the most disturbed, appreciate being shown kindness, suggests that however hardened we may become, the capacity for empathy remains.

This characteristic of appreciating others' concern is,

I believe, a reflection of our 'inability to bear the sight of another's suffering'. I say this because alongside our natural ability to empathize with others, we have also a need for others' kindness which which runs like a thread throughout our whole life. It is most apparent when we are young and when we are old. But we have only to fall ill to be reminded how important it is to be loved and cared about even during our prime years. Though it may seem a virtue to be able to do without affection, in reality a life wanting this precious ingredient must be a miserable one. It is surely not a coincidence that the lives of most criminals turn out to have been lonely and lacking in love.

We see this appreciation of kindness reflected in our response to the human smile. For me, human beings' ability to smile is one of our most beautiful characteristics. It is something no animal can do. Not dogs, nor even whales or dolphins, each of them very intelligent beings with a clear affinity for humans, can smile as we do. Personally, I always feel a bit curious when I smile at someone and they remain serious and unresponding. On the other hand, my heart is gladdened when they reciprocate. Even in the case of someone I have nothing to do with, when that person smiles at me, I am touched. But why? The answer surely is that a genuine smile touches something fundamental in us: our natural appreciation of kindness.

Indeed, so profound is our appreciation of affection

and love that it seems to begin even before our birth. According to some scientist friends of mine, there is strong evidence to suggest that a mother's mental and emotional state greatly affects the well-being of her unborn child, that it benefits her baby if she maintains a warm and gentle state of mind. A happy mother bears a happy child. On the other hand, frustration and anger are harmful to the healthy development of the baby. Similarly, during the first weeks after birth, warmth and affection continue to play a supreme role in the infant's physical development. At this stage, the brain is growing very rapidly, a function which doctors believe is somehow assisted by the constant touch of the mother or surrogate. This shows that though the baby may not know or care who is who, it has a clear physical need of affection. Perhaps, too, it explains why it is possible to imagine even the most fractious, agitated and paranoid individuals responding positively to the affection and care of others. As infants they must have been nurtured by someone.

Should a baby be neglected during this critical period, clearly it could not survive. Fortunately, this is very rarely the case. Almost without exception, the mother's first act is to offer her baby her nourishing milk – an act which to me symbolizes unconditional love. Her affection here is totally genuine and uncalculating: she expects nothing in return. As for the baby, it is drawn naturally to its mother's breast. Why? Of course we can speak of the survival instinct. But in addition I think it reasonable to conjecture a degree of affection on the part of the infant towards its mother. If it felt aversion, surely it would not suckle? And if the mother felt aversion, it is doubtful her milk would flow freely. But what we see instead is a relationship based on love and mutual tenderness which is totally spontaneous. It is not learned from others, no religion requires it, no laws impose it, no schools have taught it. It arises quite naturally.

This instinctual care of mother for child – shared it seems with many animals – is crucial in that it suggests that alongside the baby's fundamental need of love in order to survive, there exists an innate capacity on the part of the mother to give love. So powerful is it that we might almost suppose a biological component to be at work. Of course it could be argued that this reciprocal love is nothing more than a survival mechanism. That could well be so. But that is not to deny its existence. Nor indeed does it undermine my conviction that this need and capacity for love suggests that we are in fact loving by nature.

If this seems improbable, consider our differing response to kindness and to violence. Most of us find violence intimidating. Conversely, when we are shown kindness, we respond with greater trust. Similarly, consider the relationship between peace – which as we have seen is the fruit of love – and good health. According to my understanding, our constitution is more suited to peace and tranquillity than to violence and aggression. We all know that stress and anxiety can lead to high blood pressure and other negative symptoms. In the Tibetan medical system, mental and emotional disturbances are held to be a cause of many constitutional diseases, including cancer. Conversely, peace, tranquillity and others' care are essential to recovery from illness. We can also identify a basic longing for peace. Why? Because peace suggests life and growth whereas violence suggests only misery and death. This is why the idea of a Pure Land, or of Heaven, attracts us and we feel like going there. If such a place were described in terms of unending warfare and strife, we would much rather remain in this world.

Notice too how we respond to the phenomenon of life itself. When spring follows winter, the days become longer, there is more sunshine, the grass grows afresh: automatically our spirits lift. On the other hand, at the approach of winter, the leaves begin to fall one by one and much of the vegetation around us becomes as though dead. Small wonder if we tend to feel a bit downcast at that time of year. The indication here is surely that our nature prefers life over death, growth over decay, construction over destruction.

Consider also the behaviour of children. In them we see what is natural to the human character before it has been overlaid with learned ideas. We find that very young babies do not really differentiate between one person and another. They attach much more importance to the smile of the people in front of them than to anything else. Even when they start to grow up they are not much interested in differences of race, nationality, religion or family background. When they meet with other children they do not stop to discuss these things. They immediately begin the much more important business of play. Nor is this just sentimentalism. I see the reality whenever I visit one of the childrens' villages in Europe where numbers of Tibetan refugee children have been educated since the early 1960's. These villages were founded to care for orphaned children from countries at war with one another. To no one's great surprise, it was found that despite their different backgrounds, put together, these children live in complete harmony with one another.

Now it could be objected that whilst we may all share a capacity for loving-kindness, human nature is such that inevitably we tend to reserve it for those closest to us. We are biased towards our families and friends. Our feelings of concern for those outside this circle will depend very much on individual circumstances: those who feel threatened are not likely to have very much goodwill for those who threaten them. All this is true enough. Nor do I deny that whatever our capacity for fellow feeling, when our very survival is threatened, it may but rarely prevail over the instinct to self preservation. Still this does not mean that the capacity is no longer there, that the potential does not remain. Even soldiers after a battle will often help their enemies retrieve the dead and wounded.

In all of what I have said about our basic nature, I do not mean to suggest that I believe it has no negative aspects. Where there is sentience, hatred ignorance and violence do indeed arise naturally. This is why, although our nature is basically disposed towards kindness and compassion, we are all capable of cruelty and hatred. It is why we have to struggle. It also explains how individuals raised in a strictly non-violent environment have turned into the most horrible butchers. In connection with this, I recall my visit some years ago to the Washington Memorial which pays tribute to the martyrs and heroes of the Jewish Holocaust at the hands of the Nazis. The thing about the monument which struck me most forcefully was its simultaneous cataloguing of different forms of human behaviour. On one side it lists the victims of acts of unspeakable atrocity. On the other, it remembers the heroic acts of kindness on the part of Christian families and others who willingly took terrible risks in order to harbour their Jewish brothers and sisters. I felt that this was entirely appropriate, and very necessary, to show the two sides of human potential.

But the existence of this negative potential does not prove conclusively that human nature is inherently violent, or even disposed towards violence. Perhaps one of the reasons for the popularity of the belief that human nature is aggressive lies in our continual exposure to bad news through the media. Yet the very cause of this is surely that good news is not news.

To say that human nature is not only non-violent but disposed towards love and compassion, kindness, gentleness, affection, creation and so on does, of course, imply a general principle which must, by definition, be applicable to each individual human being. What then are we to say about those individuals whose lives seem to be given over wholly to violence and aggression? During the past century alone there are several obvious examples to consider. What of Hitler and his plan to exterminate the entire Jewish race? What of Stalin and his pogroms? What of Chairman Mao, the man I once knew and admired, and the barbarous insanity of the Cultural Revolution? What of Pol Pot, architect of the Killing Fields? And what about those who torture and kill for pleasure?

Here I must admit that I can think of no single explanation to account for the monstrous acts of these people. However, we must recognize two things. Firstly, such people do not come from nowhere but from within a particular society at a particular time and in particular place. Their actions need to be considered in relation to these circumstances. Secondly, we need to recognize the role of the imaginative faculty in their actions. Their schemes were and are carried out in accordance with a vision, albeit a perverted one. Notwithstanding the fact that nothing can justify the suffering they instigated, whatever their explanation might be and whatever positive intentions to which they might point, Hitler, Stalin, Mao and Pol Pot each had goals towards which he was working. If we examine those actions which are uniquely human, which animals cannot perform, we find this imaginative faculty playing a vital role. The faculty itself is a unique asset. But the use to which it is put determines whether the actions it conceives are positive or negative, ethical or unethical. The individual's motivation (*kun-long*) is thus the governing factor. Whereas a vision properly motivated – which it recognizes others' desire for and equal right to happiness and to be free of suffering – can lead to wonders, when it is divorced from basic human feeling the potential for destruction cannot be overestimated.

As for those who kill for pleasure or, worse, for no reason at all, we can only conjecture a deep submergence of the basic impulse towards care and affection for others. Still this need not mean that it is entirely extinguished. As I pointed out earlier, except perhaps in the most extreme cases, it is possible to imagine that even these people appreciate being shown affection. Their positive disposition remains.

Actually, the reader does not need to accept my proposition that human nature is basically disposed towards love and compassion to see that the capacity for empathy which underlies it is of crucial importance when it comes to ethics. We saw earlier how an ethical act is a non-harming act. But how are we to determine whether an act is genuinely non-harming? We find that in practice, if we are not able to connect with others to some extent, if we cannot at least imagine the potential impact of our actions on others, we have no means to discriminate between right and wrong, between what is appropriate and what is not, between harming and non-harming. It follows, therefore, that if we could enhance this capacity – that is to say our sensitivity towards others' suffering – the more we did so, the less we would be able to tolerate seeing others' pain and the more we would be concerned to ensure that no action of ours caused harm to others.

The fact that we can indeed enhance our capacity for empathy becomes obvious when we consider its nature. We experience it mainly as a feeling. And, as we all know, to a greater or lesser extent we can not only restrain our feelings through reasoning but we can enhance them in the same way. Our desire for objects – perhaps a new car – is enhanced by our turning it over and over in our imagination. Similarly, if we direct our mental faculties onto our feelings of empathy, we find that not only can we enhance them but we can transform them into love and compassion itself.

As such, our innate capacity for empathy is the source of that most precious of all qualities, which in Tibetan we call *nying-je*. Now whilst generally translated simply as compassion, the term *nying-je* has a wealth of meaning that is difficult to convey succinctly, though the ideas it contains are universally understood. It connotes love, affection, kindness, gentleness, generosity of spirit and warm-heartedness. It is also used as a term of both sympathy and of endearment. But most importantly, *nying-je* denotes a feeling of connection with others, reflecting its origins in empathy. Thus whilst we might say, 'I love my house' or 'I have strong feelings of affection for this place', we cannot say 'I have compassion' for these things. Having no feelings themselves, objects cannot be empathized with. We cannot therefore speak of having compassion for them.

Although it is clear from this description that *nying-je*, or love and compassion, is understood as an emotion, it belongs to that category of emotions which have a more developed cognitive component. Some emotions, such as the revulsion we tend to feel at the sight of blood are basically instinctual. Others, such as fear of poverty, have this more developed cognitive component. We can thus understand *nying-je* in terms of a combination of empathy and reason. Empathy we can think of as a very honest person; reason as someone who is very practical. When the two are put together, the combination is highly effective. As such, *nying-je* is quite different from those random feelings, like anger and lust, which, far from bringing us happiness, only trouble us and destroy our peace of mind.

This fact that we can enhance our feelings of concern for others is of supreme importance because the more we develop compassion, the more genuinely ethical our conduct will be. As we have seen, when we act out of concern for others, our behaviour towards them is automatically positive. This is because we have no room for suspicion when our hearts are filled with love. It is if an inner door is opened, allowing us to reach out. Having concern for others breaks down the impediment which inhibits healthy interaction with others. And not only that, but when our intentions towards others are good, we find that any feelings of shyness or insecurity we may have are greatly reduced. To the extent that we are able to open this inner door, we experience a sense of abandonment from our habitual preoccupation with self. Paradoxically, we find this gives rise to firm feelings of confidence. Thus, if I may give an example from my own experience, I find that whenever I meet new people and have this positive disposition, there is no barrier between us. No matter who or what they are, whether they have blonde hair or black hair, or hair that is dyed green, I feel that I am simply encountering a fellow human being with the same desire to be happy and to avoid suffering as myself. And I find that I can speak to them as if they were old friends, even at our first meeting. By keeping in mind that ultimately, we are all brothers and sisters, that there is no substantial difference between us, that all others share my desire to be happy and to avoid suffering, I can express my feelings as readily as to someone I have known intimately for years. And not just with a few nice words or gestures, but really heart to heart, no matter what the language barrier.

We also find that when we act out of concern for others, the peace this creates in our own hearts brings peace to everyone with whom we associate. We bring peace to the family, peace to our friends, to the workplace, to the community and so to the world. Why then would anyone not wish to develop this quality? Could anything be more sublime than that which brings peace and happiness to all? For my own part, the mere ability we human beings have to sing the praises of love and compassion is a most precious gift.

Conversely, not even the most sceptical reader could suppose that peace ever comes about as the result of aggressive and inconsiderate – that is to say unethical – behaviour. Of course it cannot. I well remember how I learned this particular lesson when I was a small boy in Tibet. One of my attendants, Kenrab Tenzin, had made a pet of a small parrot which he used to feed with nuts. Although he was a rather stern man with bulging eyes and a somewhat forbidding aspect, merely at the sound of his footsteps, or of his coughing, this parrot would show signs of excitement. As the bird nibbled from his fingers, Kenrab Tenzin would stroke its head – at which it appeared to enter a state of ecstasy. For my own part, I was very envious of this relationship and desired the bird to show me similar friendliness. But when I tried on a few occasions to feed it myself, I failed to get a good response. So I tried poking at it with a stick in the hope of provoking a better reaction. Needless to say the result was totally negative. Far from forcing it to behave better towards me, the bird took fright. What little prospect of founding friendly relations there may have been were totally destroyed. I learned thereby that friendships come about not as the result of bullying, but as a result of kindness and compassion.

The world's major religious traditions each give the development of love and compassion a key role. Because it is both the source and the result of patience, tolerance, forgiveness and all good qualities, its importance is considered to extend from the beginning to the end of spiritual practice. But even without a religious perspective, love and compassion are clearly of fundamental importance to us all. Given our basic premise that an ethical act is one which does not harm another's experience or expectation of happiness, it follows that we need to take others' feelings into consideration, the basis for which is our innate capacity for empathy. And as we transform this into love and compassion, through the two-pronged approach of guarding against those factors which obstruct compassion and cultivating those conducive to it, so our practice of ethics improves. This, we find, leads to happiness both for ourselves and others.

PART TWO

Ethics and the Individual

CHAPTER SIX

THE ETHICS OF
RESTRAINT

Developing the compassion on which ethical conduct – and thus happiness – depends also demands a two-pronged approach. On the one hand, we need to restrain the factors which inhibit compassion. On the other, we need to cultivate those which are conducive to it. As we have seen, the factors conducive to compassion are the spiritual qualities of love, patience, tolerance, forgiveness, humility and so on. What inhibits it is the lack of inner restraint that we have identified as the source of all unethical behaviour.

The undisciplined mind is like an elephant. If left to

blunder around out of control, it will wreak havoc. But the harm and suffering we encounter as a result of failing to restrain the negative impulses of mind far exceed the damage a rampaging elephant can cause. Not only are these impulses capable of bringing about the destruction of things, they can also be the cause of lasting pain to others and so to ourselves. By this I do not mean to suggest that the mind (*lo*) is inherently destructive. There is an important distinction to be made between consciousness as such and the thoughts and emotions it experiences. Under the influence of a strongly negative thought or emotion, the mind may seem to be characterized by a single quality. But if, for instance, hatefulness were an inherent characteristic of consciousness, then consciousness must always be hateful. Clearly this is not the case.

Similarly, whilst at the time a powerful experience may overwhelm us, it no longer troubles us when we consider it later. When very young I used to become highly excited, as the old year drew to a close, at the thought of *Monlam Chenmo*. This was the Great Prayer Festival which marked the start of the Tibetan New Year. In my capacity as Dalai Lama, I had an important role in this which meant moving from the Potala to a set of rooms in the Jokhang temple, one of Tibet's holiest shrines. As the day drew closer, I would spend more and more time daydreaming at the prospect, half-terrified and half-elated, and less and less time studying. My feelings of terror were at the thought of the long recital I had to give from memory during the main ceremony. My excitement was at the thought of passing amongst the huge crowd of pilgrims and traders thronging the market-place in front of the temple complex. Both the over-excitement and the aversion I felt then was real enough. Today, of course, I can laugh at these memories. I am now quite used to crowds. And after so many years of practice, the recitation no longer troubles me.

We can thus conceive of the nature of mind in terms of the water in a lake. When the water is stirred up by a storm, the mud from the lake's bottom clouds it, making it appear opaque. But the nature of the water is not dirty. When the storm passes, the mud settles and the water is left clear once again. So although we may generally suppose mind, or consciousness to be a monolithic entity, when we consider it more deeply, we see that it consists in a whole spectrum of events and experiences. These include our sensory perception which engages with objects directly, as well as our thoughts and feelings which are mediated by language and concepts. Consciousness is also dynamic: through deliberate engagement we can effect changes in our mental and emotional states. We know, for example, how comfort and reassurance can help dispel fear. Similarly, counselling, which leads to greater awareness, and affection can help alleviate depression. This observation is crucial. It tells us that prior to our every intended action, there must be a mental and emotional event to which we are more or less free to respond. Until we have learned to discipline our mind to some degree, we will have difficulty in exercising this freedom, however. What often determines the moral content of our acts is how and in what manner we respond to these events and experiences. In simple terms, if we do so positively, keeping others' interests before us, our acts will be positive. If we respond negatively, neglecting others, our acts will be negative and unethical.

According to this understanding, we might think of mind or consciousness in terms of a president or monarch who is very honest, very pure. Our thoughts and emotions are like cabinet ministers. Some of them give good advice, some bad. Some have the well-being of others as their principal concern, others only their own narrow interests. The responsibility of the main consciousness – the leader – is to determine which of these subordinates gives good advice and which bad; which of them are reliable and which are not, and to act on the advice of the one sort, and not the other.

Mental and emotional events which, in this sense give bad advice can themselves be described as a form of suffering. Indeed, we find that when they are allowed to develop to any significant degree, the mind becomes, as it were, swamped with emotion and we experience a kind of inner turbulence. This also has a physical dimension. In a moment of anger, for example, we experience a powerful disturbance to our habitual equilibrium which can often be sensed by others. We are all familiar with the way in which the whole atmosphere is spoiled when just one member of the household is in a bad mood. When we become enraged, both people and animals tend to avoid us. Sometimes this turbulence is so strong that we find great difficulty containing it. This may cause us to lash out at others. In doing so we externalize our inner suffering.

This is not to say that all feelings or emotions which cause us discomfort are necessarily negative. The main thing that distinguishes ordinary emotions from those which undermine peace, is their negative cognitive component. A moment of sorrow does not become disabling grief unless we hold onto it and add negative thoughts and imaginings. In the case of the over excitement I felt about these crowds of pilgrims and traders and the fear I had of the long recitation, there was an added cognitive component. Through my somewhat obsessive daydreaming, my imagination superimposed something beyond the reality of the situation. And it was this that undermined my basic serenity.

For this reason, not all fear is like the childish one I have just described. There are occasions when we experience a more rational kind of fear. Far from being negative this may actually be helpful. It can heighten our awareness and give us the energy we need to protect ourselves. On the first night of my escape from Lhasa in 1959, when I left home dressed as a soldier, I certainly felt this kind of fear. But because I had neither the time nor the inclination to think about it, it did not much unsettle me. Its main effect was to make me very alert. One could say that this was an instance of fear which was both justified and useful.

The fear we feel in relation to a situation which is quite delicate or critical, may also be justified. Here I am thinking of what we feel when we have to take a decision we know will have a material effect on others' lives. Such fear may disconcert us somewhat. But the most dangerous and negative is the type of fear that is completely unreasonable and which can totally overwhelm and paralyse us.

In Tibetan we call such negative and emotional events *nyong mong*: literally, 'that which afflicts from within' or, as the term is usually translated, 'afflictive emotion'. In Buddhist thought, every emotion has a cognitive dimension and every thought an affective dimension. Any thought, feeling or mental event that undermines our peace of mind from within – all negative thoughts and emotions such as anger, pride, lust, greed, envy and so on – are considered to be afflictions in this sense. These afflictive emotions are so strong that, if we do nothing to counter them – though there is no one who does not value their life – they can lead us to the extremes of madness and even suicide itself. We tend to imagine these negative thoughts and emotions to be an integral part of our mind about which we can do very little. Far from recognizing their destructive potential and challenging them, we often nurture and reinforce them. But as we shall see, their nature is wholly destructive. They are the very source of unethical conduct. They are also the basis of the worry, depression, confusion and stress which are such a feature of modern society.

When we analyse these negative thoughts and emotions, we begin to see that they are what obstruct our most basic aspiration: to be happy and to avoid suffering. When we act under the influence of afflictive emotion, our chief concern is not others' interest but only our own: it is thus the cause of our selfish and violent behaviour towards others. Murder, scandal and deceit all have their origin in afflictive emotion. This is why I say that the undisciplined mind is the source of all of our troubles which do not fall into the category of unavoidable suffering such as sickness, old age, death and so on. Our failure to check our response to afflictive emotions opens the door to suffering for both ourselves and others.

To say that when we cause others to suffer we ourselves suffer does not mean it is a logical entailment that in every instance when I hit someone, I will be hit myself. The proposition I am making is much more general than this. Rather, I mean to suggest that the impact of our actions – both positive and negative – registers deep within us. As we saw earlier, if it is correct that, on some level, all of us have the capacity for empathy, then this potential must be overwhelmed, or submerged in some way for an individual to harm another. In the instance of a person who cruelly tortures another, their mind (lo) must be strongly gripped at the gross, or conscious level by some kind of false thinking or ideology which causes them to believe their victim to be deserving of ill treatment. Such a belief – which to some degree must have been deliberately chosen – is what enables the cruel person to suppress their feelings. Nevertheless, deep down, there is bound to be some kind of effect. Consider in this context the example we looked at earlier of merciless dictators like Hitler and Stalin. It seems that as they neared the end of their lives, they became lonely, anxious, full of dread and suspicious of everyone, like crows afraid of their own shadows.

Of course, the number of people who go to such extremes is very small. The impact of minor negative actions is also much more subtle than major ones. So, as a less extreme example of the way in which negative actions cause suffering both to ourselves as well as others, consider a child going out to play and getting into a fight with another child. To begin with, the child who is victorious may experience a sense of satisfaction. But on returning home, that emotion will subside and a more subtle state of mind will manifest. At that point, a sense of unease sets in. This sort of feeling we could almost describe as a sense of alienation from self: the individual doesn't feel quite 'right'. In an alternate case, a child goes out to play with a friend and shares an enjoyable afternoon with that playmate. For this child there will be not only an immediate sense of satisfaction, but also a sense of calm and comfort when the mind has settled down and the excitement has worn off.

Another example of the way in which negative actions harm the one who indulges them can be seen in the context of an individual's reputation. Given that by nature, it seems, we humans – even for that matter animals – abhor meanness, aggressiveness and deceit, it follows that if we engage in activities which harm others, despite the temporary satisfaction we might gain thereby, people will at some point begin to look askance at us. On account of our bad reputation, they will become apprehensive, nervous and suspicious of us. In time, we will start to lose friends. In this way, because a good reputation is a source of happiness, we bring suffering on ourselves if we spoil it.

Indeed, though there may be a few exceptions, we find that if a person lives a very selfish life, without concern for others' welfare, this person tends to become quite lonely and miserable. Though they may be surrounded by people who are friends of their wealth or status, when the selfish or aggressive individual faces tragedy, not only do these so-called friends vanish, they may even secretly rejoice. Moreover, if these individuals are actively malicious too, it is likely that when they die they will not be much missed. Again, people may actually be glad – as many of the inmates of the Nazi death camps must have been glad at the subsequent execution of their captors. Conversely, we find that people who are actively concerned for others are much respected, even venerated. When such as these die, many mourn and regret their passing. Consider the case of Mahatma Gandhi. Despite a Western education, and the opportunities it gave him to lead a comfortable life, he chose out of consideration for others to live in India almost as a beggar in order to devote himself to his life's work. Though his name is now just a memory, millions still draw comfort and inspiration from his noble deeds.

We can point to a number of different factors as the actual cause of afflictive emotion. These include our habitual self-centredness, as well as our tendency to project characteristics onto things and events above and beyond what actually is there. (Here we see our creative faculties in play.) Because our negative thoughts and emotions do not exist independently of other phenomena, the very objects and events we come into contact with themselves play a contributory role. Thus, there is nothing which does not have the potential to trigger them. Anything can be a source of afflictive emotion – not just our adversaries but our friends and our most valued possessions too, even ourselves.

This suggests that the first step in the process of actually countering our negative thoughts and emotions is to avoid the situations and activities which would normally give rise to them. If, for example, we find we become angry whenever we meet with a particular person, it may be best to keep away from them until our internal resources are more developed. The second step is to avoid the actual conditions which lead to these strong negative thoughts and emotions. This, however, presupposes that we have learned to recognize afflictive emotions as they arise in us. This is not always easy. For, whilst hatred is a very strong emotion when fully developed, in its beginning stages the aversion we feel towards a particular object or event may be quite subtle. And even at their most advanced stages of development, negative thoughts and emotions do not always manifest themselves dramatically. The assassin may be relatively calm in the moment that he pulls the trigger.

To this end, we need to pay close attention and be aware of our body and its actions, of our speech and what we say, and of our hearts and minds and what we think and feel. We must be on the look out for the slightest negativity and keep asking ourselves such questions as 'What is the nature of consciousness? Is it it existent in and of itself, or does it exist in dependence on other factors?', 'Am I happier when my thoughts and emotions are negative and destructive or when they are wholesome?' We need to think, think, think. We should be like a scientist who collects data, analyses it, and draws the appropriate conclusion. Gaining insight into our negative thoughts and emotions is a long-term endeavour, and one which is capable of almost infinite refinement. But unless we undertake it, we will be unable to see where to make the necessary changes in our lives.

Were we to expend even a fraction of the time and effort we expend in trivial activities – pointless gossip and the like – on gaining insight into the actual nature of afflictive emotion, I believe it would have a huge impact on our quality of life. Both individuals and society would benefit. One of the first things we would discover is how destructive afflictive emotions are. The more we develop an appreciation of their destructive nature, the more we become disinclined to act under their influence. This alone would have a positive effect on our lives.

Consider that not only do negative thoughts and emotions destroy our experience of peace. They also undermine our health. At least so far as the Tibetan medical system is concerned, anger is a primary source of many illnesses, including for example those associated with high blood pressure, sleeplessness and degenerative disorders – a view which seems to be increasingly accepted in allopathic medicine.

Another childhood memory illustrates the way in which negative thoughts and emotions destructively affect our hearts and minds as well. When I was a teenager, one of my favourite pastimes was tinkering with the old cars that my predecessor, the Thirteenth Dalai Lama, had acquired not long before he died in 1933. There were four of them, two baby Austins of British manufacture, a Dodge and a beaten-up jeep, both of American origin. Together they comprised almost the only powered vehicles in all Tibet. For the young Dalai Lama, these dusty relics held an irresistible attraction and I longed to have them running again. My secret dream was actually to learn to drive. But it was only after a lot of pestering of various government officials that finally I found someone who knew anything about mechanics. This was Lhakba Tsering, who came from Kalimpong, a town just over the border with India. One day, I recall, he was working on the engine of one of the cars when, dropping his spanner, he shouted an oath and stood up abruptly. Unfortunately, he had forgotten that the bonnet was open above him and he hit his head with a terrible crack. To my great surprise, instead of extracting himself carefully, he become further enraged and straightening up again, hit his head even harder a second time. For a moment, I stood astonished at these antics. Then I found I could not stop laughing.

Lhakba Tsering's outburst resulted in nothing more than two generous bruises. That was merely unfortunate for him. But from this we see how the afflictive emotions destroy one of our most precious qualities, namely our capacity for discriminative awareness. Robbed of the ability which enables us to judge between right and wrong, to evaluate what is likely to be of lasting benefit and what of merely temporary benefit to self and others, and to discern the likely outcome of our actions, we are no better off than animals. Small wonder that, under the influence of afflictive emotion, we do what we ordinarily would never consider doing.

This obliteration of our critical faculties points to another negative characteristic of this type of mental and emotional event. It deceives us. It seems to offer satisfaction, but does not provide it. Take lust, for example. It promises happiness, but the best it can provide us with is temporary satiety. Moreover, by blinding our critical faculties, lust causes us to ignore the impact of our actions on others such that by the time we realize our mistake, it may be too late to prevent actions which lead to suffering – for our spouses or children, for example. Lust is also especially difficult to deal with in that sexual attraction is a tremendously powerful force. As human beings, we are naturally attracted to external objects, whether it be through the eyes where we are attracted by form, through the ears where the attraction arises in relation to sound, or through any of the other senses. Each of them has the potential to be a source of difficulty for us. Yet sexual attraction involves all five senses. As a result, when desire is also present, it has the ability to cause us enormous problems. This fact is recognized in the ethical directives against sexual misconduct articulated by every major religion and which, at least in the Buddhist tradition, are a reminder of the tendency for sexual desire to become obsessive. It can quickly reach the point where a person has almost no room left for constructive activity. These precepts also reflect an intuition that relationships founded primarily on sexual attraction are almost always unstable.

The afflictive emotions also have an irrational dimension. They encourage us to suppose that appearances are invariably commensurate with reality. When we become angry or feel hatred, we tend to relate to others as if their characteristics were immutable. A person can appear to be objectionable from the crown of their head to the soles of their feet. We forget that they, like us, are merely suffering human beings with the same wish to be happy and to avoid suffering as we ourselves – even though common sense tells us that when the force of our anger diminishes they are sure to seem a little better at least. The same is true in reverse if individuals become infatuated. The other appears to be wholly desirable – until such time as the grip of afflictive emotion subsides and they come to seem a little less than perfect. Indeed when our passions become so strongly aroused, there is considerable danger of going to the opposite extreme. The once-idolized individual comes to seem despicable and hateful – though, of course, it is the same person throughout.

The afflictive emotions are also useless. The more we give in to them, the less room we have for our good qualities, such as kindness and compassion, and the less able we are to solve our problems. Indeed, there is no occasion in which these disturbing thoughts and emotions are helpful, either to ourselves or to others.

The more angry we are, the more people shun us. The more suspicious we are, the more cut off from people we become and thus the more lonely. The more lustful we are, the less we are able to develop proper relationships with others and, again, the more lonely we become. Consider the individual whose activities are directed principally by afflictive emotion or, to put it another way, by gross attachments and aversions: by greed, arrogant ambition and so forth. Such a person may become very powerful and very famous. His or her name may even go down in history. But after these individuals die, their power is gone and their fame is no more than an empty word. So what have they really achieved?

Nowhere is the inutility of afflictive emotion more obvious than in the case of anger. When we become angry, we stop being compassionate, loving, generous, forgiving, tolerant and patient altogether. We thus deprive ourselves of the very things in which happiness consists. Not only does anger immediately destroy our critical faculties, it tends inevitably towards rage, spite, hatred, malice and conceit – each of which is always negative in that each is a direct cause of harm to others. As such, anger has no use but to cause suffering. At the very least it causes the pain of embarrassment. For example, I have always enjoyed repairing watches. But I can recall a number of occasions as a boy when I completely lost my patience with those tiny, intricate parts. I picked up the mechanism and smashed it down on the table. Of course, I later felt very sorry and ashamed at my behaviour – especially on the one occasion, I had to return the watch to its owner in a worse condition than it was in before.

This story, trivial in itself, also makes the point that, though we may have an abundance of material wealth – good food, fine furnishings, a nice television set – when we become angry, we lose all inner peace. We no longer enjoy even our breakfast. If afflictive emotion becomes habitual, we may be ever so learned, rich, or powerful, but others will simply avoid us. They will say 'Oh yes, he is very clever, but he has such bad moods you know' and people will keep away. Or they will say 'Yes she is extraordinarily talented, but she gets upset so easily. You had better watch out'. Just as when a dog is always growling and showing its teeth, we are cautious of those whose hearts are disturbed by anger. We would rather forgo their company than risk an outburst.

I do not deny that, as in the case of fear, there is a kind of 'raw' anger that we experience more as a rush of energy than as a cognitively enhanced emotion. Conceivably this form of anger could have positive consequences. It is not impossible to imagine anger at the sight of injustice caus- ing someone to act altruistically. The anger that causes us to go to the assistance of someone being attacked in the street could be characterized as positive. But if this goes beyond meeting the injustice and becomes personal and turns into vengefulness or maliciousness, then danger arises. We need to be careful that we distinguish between the action and agent – as we generally do in the case of our own acts. The fact that we often fail to do this when it comes to others points to the unreliability even of justifiable anger. In fact, although such emotion comes to us in the guise of a protector, as it were, giving us boldness and strength, we find that this energy is essentially blind. Decisions taken under its influence are often a source of regret. More often than not, such anger is actually an indication of weakness rather than of strength. There can be few people who have not experienced an argument which has deteriorated to the point at which one person at least is reduced to general abuse: a clear sign of the weakness of their position. Moreover, we do not need anger to develop courage and confidence. As we shall see, it can be done through other means.

Should it still seem too much to say that anger is an entirely useless emotion, we can ask ourselves who says anger can bring happiness? Nobody. Which doctor prescribes anger as treatment for any disease? There isn't one. Anger can only hurt us. It has nothing to recommend it. Let the reader ask himself or herself: when we become angry, do we feel happy? Does our mind become calmer and our body relax? Or is it the case that we feel tense in body and unsettled of mind?

If we are to retain our peace of mind and thereby our happiness, it follows that alongside a more rational and disinterested approach to our negative thoughts and emotions, we must cultivate a strong habit of restraint in response to them. Negative thoughts and emotions are what cause us to act unethically. It is inevitable that those we live amongst will turn against us and prevent us from being happy unless we cultivate this restraint. Furthermore, because afflictive emotion is also the source of internal suffering in that it is the basis of doubt, confusion, insecurity, worry and the very loss of self-respect which undermines our sense of confidence, failure to cultivate restraint means that we will remain in a state of mental and emotional discomfort. Inner peace will be impossible. In place of happiness there will be insecurity. Anxiety and depression will never be far away.

Cultivating a habit of inner restraint is, of course, a major undertaking, but at least we are familiar with the principle. For example, knowing its destructive potential, we restrain ourselves and our children from indulging in drug abuse. However, it is important to recognize that restraining our response to negative thoughts and emotions involves more than just suppressing them. This is why insight into their destructive nature is crucial. Merely knowing that envy is potentially a very powerful and destructive emotion – perhaps because some authority figure tells us so – cannot provide a strong defence against the insistence of desire. If we order our lives externally but ignore the inner dimension, inevitably we will find that doubt, anxiety and other afflictions develop, and happiness will elude us. This is because, unlike physical discipline, true inner – or spiritual – discipline cannot be achieved by force but only through voluntary and deliberate effort. In other words, conducting ourselves ethically consists in more than merely obeying laws and precepts.

Some people may feel that although it may be right to curb the feelings of intense hatred which can cause us to be violent and even to kill, we are in danger of losing our independence when we restrain our emotions and discipline the mind. Actually, the opposite is true. When we indulge our negative thoughts and feelings, inevitably we become accustomed to them. As a result, gradually we become more and more prone to them. The trouble here is that, though they may be purely internal events to begin with, they cannot fail to be expressed as soon as external circumstances seem to warrant. This is why it is important to tackle our negative thoughts and emotions as close to the source as possible. At the causal level, we have much greater opportunities to change their course, before the necessary causes and conditions are fully met. Whereas if we delay, it becomes almost impossible to prevent them from coming to fruition in negative deeds. Like their counterparts of love and compassion, anger and the afflictive emotions can never be used up. They have, rather, a propensity to increase, like a river flooding in summer when the snow melts, such that far from being free, our minds are enslaved and rendered helpless by them.

In fact, when we think properly, it is totally illogical to seek happiness if we do nothing to restrain angry, spiteful and malicious thoughts and emotions. Inner peace, which is the principal characteristic of happiness, and anger cannot coexist without one undermining the other. Indeed, negative thoughts and emotions undermine the very causes of peace and happiness. Consider that when we become angry, we often use harsh words. Harsh words can destroy friendship. Therefore, given that happiness arises in the context of our relations with others, if we destroy friendships, we undermine one of the very conditions of happiness itself.

To say that we need to curb anger and afflictive emotion does not mean that we should deny our feelings. There is an important distinction to be made between denial and restraint. The latter constitutes a deliberate and voluntarily adopted discipline based on appreciation of the benefits of restraint. This is very different from the case of someone who suppresses emotions such as anger out of a felt need to present a facade of self-control, or out of fear of what others may think. Such behaviour is a bit like closing a wound which is still infected. Again, we are not talking about rule-following. Indeed, where denial and suppression occur, this can certainly lead to individuals storing up anger and resentment which at some future point they are unable to contain.

In other words, there are of course thoughts and emotions which it is appropriate, even important to express openly – including negative ones – and there are more or less appropriate ways to express one's feelings. It is far better to confront a person or situation than to hide our anger away, brood and nurture resentment in our hearts. The important thing is to be discriminating, both in terms of the feelings we express and in how we express them. But if we do not first exercise restraint and simply let out each of them as they come to us on the grounds that they must be articulated, there is a strong possibility, for all the reasons I have given, of reaching excess and losing control.

Genuine happiness is characterized by inner peace. This arises in the context of our relationships with others. It therefore depends on ethical conduct which in its turn consists in acts which take others' well-being into account. What obstructs us from engaging in such compassionate conduct is afflictive emotion. If we wish to be happy, we need therefore to curb our response to negative thoughts and emotions. This is what I mean when I say that we must tame the wild elephant that is the undisciplined mind. We are not talking about Buddha here, we are not talking about God. We are merely recognizing that my interests and future happiness are closely connected to those of others'. When I fail to restrain my response to afflictive emotion, my actions become unethical and obstruct the conditions of my happiness.

CHAPTER SEVEN

THE ETHICS OF VIRTUE

I have suggested that, if we are to be genuinely happy, inner restraint is indispensable. We cannot stop at restraint, however. Though it may prevent us from performing any grossly negative misdeeds, mere restraint is insufficient if we are to attain that happiness which is characterised by inner peace. In order to transform ourselves – our habits and dispositions – such that all our actions are compassionate, it is necessary to develop what we might call an ethics of virtue. As well as refraining from negative thoughts and emotions, we need to cultivate and reinforce our positive qualities. Which positive qualities? Those that are conducive to compassion.

The chief of these is that which in Tibetan we call *sö-pa*. Once again, we have here a term for which there appears to be no ready equivalent in a modern language, though the ideas it conveys are universal. Often, *sö-pa* is translated simply as patience, though its literal meaning is 'able to bear' or 'able to withstand'. But with this there is also a notion of resolution. It thus denotes a deliberate response (as opposed to an unreasoned reaction) to the strong negative thoughts and emotions that tend to arise when we encounter harm. As such, *sö-pa* is that which provides us with the strength to resist suffering and protects us from losing our compassion for those who would harm us.

In this context, I am reminded of the example of Lopon-la, a monk from Namgyal, the Dalai Lama's own monastery. Following my escape from Tibet in 1959, Lopon-la was one of many thousands of monks and officials imprisoned by the occupying forces. When finally he was released, he was allowed to come to India where he rejoined his old monastery. More than twenty years after last seeing him, I found Lopon-la much as I remembered him. He looked older, of course, but physically he was unscathed. And mentally his ordeal had not affected him adversely at all. His gentleness and serenity remained. From our conversation, I learned that he had nevertheless endured grievous treatment during those long years of imprisonment. In common with all others, he had been subjected to 're-education', during which he had been forced to denounce his religion and, on many occasions, tortured as well. When I asked him whether he had ever been afraid, he admitted that there was one thing that had scared him: the possibility that he might lose the compassion and concern he felt for his jailers.

I was very moved at this, and also very inspired. Hearing Lopon-la's story confirmed what I had always believed. It is not just a person's physical constitution, nor their intelligence, nor their education nor even their social and cultural conditioning which enables them to withstand hardship. Much more significant is the individual's spiritual state. And whilst some may be able to survive through sheer willpower, the ones who suffer the least are those who attain a high level of *sö-pa*.

Forbearance and also fortitude – in the sense of courage in the face of adversity – are two words which come quite close to describing *sö-pa* at a basic level. When a person develops it, there is composure in adversity, a sense of being unperturbed, reflecting a voluntary acceptance of hardship in pursuit of a higher, spiritual aim. One of the things this involves is accepting the reality of a given situation through recognizing the vastly complex web of interrelated causes and conditions that underlie its particularity.

According to this understanding, *sö-pa* is the means by which we practise true non violence. It is what enables us to refrain from physical reactions when we are provoked, and to let go of our negative thoughts and emotions, too. We cannot speak of *sö-pa* if we give in to someone grudgingly or resentfully. For example, if a superior in the work place upsets us yet we are obliged to defer to them despite our feelings. Only if we are genuinely undisturbed can we do so. Conversely, if we find ourselves annoyed or provoked by a person over whom we have power of some sort, or by someone who could not harm us even if they wanted to – and we forbear – then, certainly, *sö-pa* is present. In other words, the one who practises patient forbearance is determined not to give in to his or her negative impulses (which are experienced as afflictive emotion in the form of anger, hatred, desire for revenge and so on) but rather counters their sense of injury and does not return harm for harm.

None of the foregoing should be taken to imply that there are not times when it is appropriate to respond to others with strong measures. Nor does practising patience in the sense I have described it mean that we must accept whatever people would do to us and simply give in. Nor again does it mean that we should never act at all when we meet with harm. *Sö-pa* is not to be confused with mere passivity. On the contrary, adopting vigorous countermeasures may be compatible with the practice of *sö-pa*. There are times in everyone's life when, in order to stop another from doing something foolish, harsh words – or even physical intervention – are required. By safeguarding our inner composure, *sö-pa* means we are in a stronger position to judge an appropriately non-violent response than if we are overwhelmed by negative thoughts and emotions. From this, we see that it is the very opposite of cowardice. Cowardice arises when we lose all confidence as a result of fear. Conversely, patient forbearance means that we remain firm even if we are afraid.

Nor, when I speak of acceptance, do I mean that we should not do everything in our power to solve our problems whenever they can be solved. In the case of present suffering – that which we are already enduring – acceptance can help ensure that the experience is not compounded by the additional burden of mental and emotional suffering. For example, there is nothing much we can do about old age. Far better to accept our condition than to fret about it. Indeed, it always strikes me as a bit foolish when very old people deny that they need help when plainly they do.

Patient forbearance, then, is the quality which enables us to prevent negative thoughts and emotions from taking hold of us. It safeguards our peace of mind in the face of adversity. Through practising patience in this way our conduct is rendered ethically wholesome. As we have seen, the first step in ethical practice is to check our response to negative thoughts and emotions as they arise. The next step – after we apply the brakes – is to counter that provocation with patience, or *so-pa*.

Here the reader may object that surely there will

be occasions when this is impossible? What about the times when someone we are close to, who knows all our weaknesses, behaves towards us in such a way that we find ourselves unable to prevent anger from completely over-whelming our defences? Under such circumstances, we may indeed find it impossible to preserve our compassion for the other. But at least we should take care not to react violently, or aggressively. Leaving the room and going for a walk, or even counting twenty breaths may be the best thing. Find some means of calming down a bit. This is why we need to put the practice of patience at the heart of our daily lives. It is a question of familiarizing ourselves with it, at the deepest level, such that when we do find ourselves in a difficult situation, although we may have to make an extra effort, we know what is involved. If we ignore the practice of patience until we are actually experiencing trouble, it is quite likely we will not succeed in resisting provocation.

One of the best ways to begin familiarizing ourselves the virtue of patience, or *sö-pa* is by taking time to reflect systematically on its benefits. Amongst those we might consider is the fact that patience has no equal in pro-tecting our concern for others, whatever their behaviour towards us. It is also the source of forgiveness itself. When *sö-pa* is combined with our ability to discriminate between action and agent, forgiveness arises naturally. It also enables us to reserve our judgement towards the act. And towards the individual, it enables us to be compassionate.

Similarly, when we develop the ability to patiently forbear, we find that we develop a proportionate reserve of
calmness and tranquillity. We tend to be less antagonistic
and more pleasant to associate with. This in turn creates
a positive atmosphere around us which makes it easy
for others to relate to us. By being better grounded
emotionally through the practice of patience, we find
that not only do we become much stronger mentally and
spiritually but we tend also to be healthier physically.
Certainly, I attribute the good health I enjoy to a generally
calm and peaceful mind.

But the most important benefit of *sö-pa* or patience
consists in the way it acts as a powerful antidote to
the affliction of anger, this being, as we have seen,
the greatest threat to our inner peace – and therefore
our happiness. Indeed, we find that patience is the best
means we have of defending ourselves internally from
its destructive effects. Consider: riches are no defence
against anger. Nor is a person's education, no matter how
accomplished and intelligent he or she may be. Nor, for
that matter, can the law be of any help. And fame is
useless. Only the inner protection of patient forbearance
can keep us from experiencing the turmoil of negative
thoughts and emotions. The mind, or spirit is not physical.
It cannot be touched or harmed directly. Only negative
thoughts and emotions can harm it. Therefore, only the
corresponding positive quality can protect it.

As a second step to familiarize ourselves with the virtue

of patience, it is also very helpful to think of adversity not so much as a threat to our peace of mind, but rather as the very means by which patience it is attained. From this perspective, we see that those who would harm us are in a sense teachers of patience. Such people teach us what we could never learn merely from hearing someone speak, be they ever so wise or holy. No more can the reader hope to learn virtue merely by reading this book – unless of course it is so boring as to demand perseverance! From adversity we can, however, learn the value of patient forbearance. And in particular those who would harm us give us unparalleled opportunities to practise ethically disciplined behaviour.

This is not to say that if others harm us they are not responsible for their actions. But let us remember that they may be acting largely out of ignorance. A child brought up in a violent environment may not know any other way to behave. As result, the question of blame is rendered largely redundant. The appropriate response to someone who causes us to suffer – and here, of course, I am not referring to those instances in which others oppose us legitimately, as when, for example, they refuse to give in to our unreasonable demands – is to recognize that they will ultimately lose their peace of mind, their inner balance and thereby their happiness by harming us. We do best if we have compassion for them, especially since a simple wish to see them hurt cannot actually harm them. It will certainly harm us, though.

Here, imagine two neighbours in dispute. One of them is able to take this dispute lightly. The other is obsessed with it and constantly schemes to find a way to hurt his or her opponent. But what happens? Nurturing malice, it will not be long before the one who broods begins to suffer. He or she will lose their appetite, then their sleep. Eventually, their health begins to go. He or she passes their days and nights in misery – with the result that ironically, they end up fulfilling the wishes of their adversary.

In fact, when we really think about it, there is something not fully rational about singling out individual persons as the objects of our anger. Here, let us conduct a simple thought experiment. Consider that in the case of someone abusing us verbally, if we feel inclined to anger on account of the pain this causes us, the focus of our feelings should really be on the words themselves since these are what is actually causing us pain. Yet we become angry with the individual shouting at us. It could be objected that since it is the person who is doing the shouting that individual is the cause of our pain. We are justified in becoming angry with them. But if this is the case, should we not direct our anger towards what drove that person to abuse us towards their afflictive emotions? For if the person were calm and at peace, they would not act in this way. Yet of these three factors, the words which hurt, the person uttering them, and the negative impulses which drive them, it is towards the person that we direct our anger. There is something inconsistent in this.

If it is objected that it is the evil nature of the one who is abusing us which is truly the cause of our pain, still we would have no reasonable grounds for anger with that individual. For if it were that person's ultimate nature to be hostile towards us, he or she would be incapable of behaving differently. In that case, anger towards them would be pointless. If we are burned, there is no sense being angry with fire. It is in the nature of fire to burn. But to remind ourselves that the notion of inherent hostility or inherent evil is false, let us observe that under different circumstances, the same person who is causing us pain could become a good friend. It is not unusual to hear of soldiers on opposing sides during conflict becoming close in peacetime. And most of us have had the experience of meeting someone who, despite a bad reputation in the past, turns out to be quite pleasant.

Of course, I do not suggest that in every situation we should engage in such reflections as these. If we are physically threatened we might do better to concentrate our energies not on reasoning like this but in running away! But what is helpful is to spend time familiarizing ourselves with the various aspects and benefits of patience. This will enable us to meet the challenges posed by adversity in a constructive manner.

I mentioned earlier the way that *sö-pa*, or patience, acts as a counterforce to anger. In fact, for every negative state, we find that we can identify one which opposes it. For example, humility opposes pride; contentment opposes greed; perseverance opposes indolence. If, therefore, we wish to overcome the unwholesome states which arise when negative thoughts and emotions are allowed to develop, cultivating virtue should not be seen as separate from restraining our response to afflictive emotion. They go hand in hand. This is why ethical discipline cannot be confined either to mere restraint or to mere affirmation of positive qualities.

To see how this process of restraint coupled with counteraction works, here let us consider anxiety. This we can describe as a form of fear, but one with a well-developed mental component. Whilst something we may have good reason to feel concerned about causes the initial loss of confidence, unless we stop and counter this fear with confidence, the imagination tends to add its negative reflections and we begin to worry. The more we indulge in worry, the more reasons we find for it, to the extent that eventually we find ourselves in a state of permanent distress. The more developed this state, the less we are able to take action against it and the stronger it becomes. But when we think carefully, we see that underlying this state is a principle narrowness of vision and a lack of proper perspective. This causes us to ignore the fact that things and events come into being as the result of innumerable different causes and conditions. We tend to concentrate on just one or two aspects of our situation. But in so doing, we inevitably restrict ourselves to finding means to overcome only these aspects. The trouble with this is if we are unable to do so, we are then in danger of becoming totally demoralized and losing all confidence. Thus, although confidence is what is lacking, the first step in overcoming anxiety is to develop a proper perspective of our situation.

This we can do in a number of different ways. One of the most effective is to try to shift the focus of attention away from self and towards others. When we succeed in this, we find that the scale of our problems diminishes. This is not to say that we should ignore our own needs altogether, but rather that we should try to remember others' needs as well, no matter how pressing ours may be. This is essential. Because when our concern for others is translated into action, we find that confidence arises automatically. Indeed, we find that almost all the mental and emotional suffering which is such a feature of modern living – including the sense of hopelessness and of loneliness – lessen the moment we begin to engage in actions motivated by concern for others. At the same time, this explains why merely performing outwardly positive actions will not suffice. Where the underlying motive is only to further one's short-term aims, we only add to our problems.

What, though, of those occasions when we find our whole lives unsatisfactory, or when we feel on the point of being overwhelmed by our problems – as happens to us all in varying degrees from time to time? When this occurs, it is vital that we make every effort to find a way of lifting our spirits. This we can do by recollecting our good fortune. We may, for example, be loved by someone; we may have certain talents; we may have received a good education; we may have our basic needs fulfilled – food to eat, clothes to wear, somewhere to live; we may have performed certain altruistic deeds in the past. Like a banker who collects interest even on the smallest amounts of money he has out on loan, we must take into consideration even the slightest positive aspect of our lives. For if we fail to find some way of uplifting ourselves, there is every danger of sinking further into our sense of powerlessness. This can lead us to believe that we have no capacity whatever for doing good. Thus we create the conditions of despair itself. At that point, suicide may come to seem the only option.

In most cases of hopelessness and despair, we find that it is the individual's perception of his or her situation rather than its reality which is the issue. Certainly, it may not be resolvable without others' co-operation. In that case it becomes a matter of asking for help. However, there may indeed be some circumstances which are hopeless. This is where religious belief can be a source of comfort – but that is a separate issue.

What else might an ethics of virtue consist in? As a general principle, it is essential to avoid extremes. Just as when we eat too much, we invite trouble no less surely than if we eat too little. So it is in the pursuit and practise of virtue. We find that even noble causes, when carried to extremes, can become a source of harm. Similarly, courage taken to excess and without due regard for circumstances quickly becomes foolhardiness. Indeed, excess undermines one of the principle purposes of practising virtue which is to offset our tendency for extreme mental and emotional reactions to others and to those events which cause us unavoidable suffering.

It is also important to realize that transforming the heart and mind (*lo*) in order that our actions become spontaneously ethical requires us to put the pursuit of virtue at the heart of our daily lives. This is because love and compassion, patience, generosity, humility, and so on are all complementary. Because it is so difficult to eradicate afflictive emotions, it is necessary that we habituate ourselves to their opposites even before negative thoughts arise. The cultivation of generosity is essential to counteract our tendency to meanness, which is grounded in self-centredness.

The most effective way of doing this in the beginning is through the practice of giving. This helps us to overcome our habit of miserliness which we tend to justify by asking 'What will I have for myself if I start giving things away?' Giving to the poor is recognized as a virtue in every major religion and in every civilized society and it clearly benefits both the giver and the receiver. The one who receives is relieved from the pangs of want. The one who gives can take comfort from the joy his or her gift brings to others. At the same time, we must recognize that there are different types and degrees of giving. If we give with the underlying motive of inflating the image others have of us, to gain renown or to make others think of us as virtuous or holy, we defile the act. In this instance, what we are practising is not generosity but self-aggrandizement. Similarly, the one who gives much may not be so generous as the one who gives little. It all depends on the giver's means and motivation.

Though not a substitute, giving of our time and energy may represent a somewhat higher order of giving than making gifts. Here I am thinking especially of the gift of service to those with mental or physical disabilities, to the homeless, to those who are lonely, to those in prison and those who have been in prison. But this type of giving also includes, for example, teachers imparting their knowledge to students. In all forms of giving, the key factor for maximum benefit for both giver and receiver is to give without any thought or expectation of reward, and to ensure that it is grounded in genuine concern for others. The more we can expand our focus to include others' interests alongside our own, the more securely we build the foundations of our own happiness.

To say that humility is an essential ingredient in our pursuit of transformation may seem to be at odds with what I have said about the need for confidence. Just as there is clearly a distinction to be made between valid confidence in the sense of self-esteem, and conceit — which we can describe as an inflated sense of importance grounded in a false image of self – so it is important to distinguish between genuine humility, which is a species of modesty, and a lack of confidence. They are not the same thing at all, though it seems that many confuse them. That this is so may go some way towards explaining why humility is now often thought of as a weakness, rather than as an indication of inner strength – especially in the context of business and professional life. Certainly modern society does not accord it the place it had in Tibet when I was young. Then, both our culture and peoples' basic admiration of humility provided a climate in which it flourished. (Conversely ambition – to be differentiated from the entirely appropriate aspiration to succeed in wholesome tasks – was seen as a quality which led all too easily to selfishness.) Yet in contemporary life, humility is more important than ever. The more successful we humans become, as individuals and as a family through our development of science and technology, the more essential it is to preserve it. For the greater our temporal achievements, the more vulnerable we become to pride and arrogance.

One helpful technique to overcome our tendency to conceit is to reflect on the example of those whose self-importance makes them an object of ridicule to others. They may not be aware of how foolish they look, but it is plain to everyone else. This is not a matter of sitting in judgement on others, however. It is a question of bringing home to ourselves, the negative consequences of such states of heart and mind. By seeing where they lead, we will be all the more determined to avoid them. In a sense, we are reversing the principle of not harming others on the basis that we ourselves do not wish to be harmed and making use of the fact that it is much easier to identify others' faults than it is to acknowledge their virtues.

Another helpful method to promote humility is to reflect on our own shortcomings. In my own case, for example, I have only to think about computers to be reduced to a state of total bewilderment! Here I should perhaps add that if humility is not to be confused with lack of confidence, it has still less to do with a sense of worthlessness.

Lack of a proper recognition of one's own value is always harmful and can lead to a state of mental, emotional and spiritual paralysis. Under such circumstances, the individual may even come to hate themselves, although I must admit that the concept of self-hatred seemed incoherent when it was first explained to me by some Western psychologists. It seemed to contradict the principle that our fundamental desire is to be happy and to avoid suffering. But I do now accept that, when a person loses all sense of perspective, there is a danger of this happening. Yet we all have the capacity for empathy. We all, therefore, have the potential to engage in wholesome conduct even if this only takes the form of positive thoughts. To suppose ourselves worthless is simply incorrect.

Another way to avoid the narrowing of vision that can

lead to such extreme states as self-hatred and despair is to rejoice in others' good fortune where we find it. As part of this practice, it is helpful to take every opportunity to show our respect for others, even to encourage them with praise when it seems appropriate. If such praise seems likely to come across as flattery or to make them feel proud, it may of course be better to keep our goodwill private. And when it is ourselves who are being praised, it is vital not to let this make us feel puffed-up and important. Instead let us merely recognize the other's generosity in appreciating our good qualities.

As a means of overcoming negative feelings towards ourselves that arise in connection with occasions in the past in which we have neglected others' feelings and indulged in our own selfish desires and interests at the expense of others, it is very helpful to develop an attitude of repentance. Here though, the reader should not suppose that I am advocating the sense of guilt about which so many of my Western friends speak. We do not seem to have a word in Tibetan that translates this word exactly. And because of its strong cultural associations, I am not certain that I have understood the concept to its fullest extent. Whilst it is natural and to be expected that we should have feelings of discomfort in relation to our past misdeeds, it seems to me that there is sometimes an element of self-indulgence when this is extended to feelings of guilt. It makes no sense to brood on the negative actions we have committed in the past. If the person is a believer in God, the appropriate action is to find some means of reconciliation. Insofar as Buddhist practice is concerned, there are various rites and practices for purification. If the individual has no religious beliefs, however, it is surely a matter of acknowledging any negative feelings we may have in relation to our misdeeds and developing a sense of sorrow and regret for them. Rather than stop at mere sorrow and regret, it is important to use this as the basis for resolution and a deep-seated commitment. Firstly never again to harm others and, secondly, to direct our actions all the more determinedly to the benefit of others. In this, the act of disclosure or confession of our negative actions to another – especially to someone we really respect and trust – is found to be very helpful. Above all, we should remember that as long as we retain the capacity of concern for others, the potential for transformation remains. We are quite wrong if we merely acknowledge the gravity of our actions inwardly and then, instead of confronting our feelings, give up all hope and do nothing. This only compounds the error.

We have a saying in Tibet that engaging in the practice of virtue is as hard as driving donkey uphill, whereas engaging in destructive activities is as easy as rolling boulders downhill. It is also said that negativities arise spontaneously as rain and gather momentum just like water following the course of gravity. What makes matters worse is our tendency to laziness. We indulge negative thoughts and emotions even while agreeing that we should not. It is essential, therefore, to address directly our tendency to put things off and while away our time in meaningless activities and to shrink from the challenge of transforming our habits on the grounds that it is too great a task. In particular, it is important not to allow ourselves to be put off by the magnitude of others' suffering. The misery of millions is not a cause for pity. Rather it is a cause for compassion.

We must also see the harm and futility of wasting our time in senseless gossip and allowing ourselves to be distracted from the task of spiritual transformation by purely worldly affairs. We must recognize that the failure to act when it is clear that action is required may itself be a negative action. Where inaction is due to anger or malice or envy, clearly afflictive emotion can be cited as the motivating factor. This is as true of simple things as it is of more complex situations. If a husband does not warn his wife that a plate she is about to pick up is hot because he desires her to be burned, clearly afflictive emotion is present. On the other hand, where inaction is simply the result of indolence, the mental and emotional state of the individual may not be so gravely negative. But the consequence may still be very serious. It is important that we are no less determined to overcome our habitual tendency to laziness than we are to exercise restraint in response to afflictive emotion.

This is no easy task, and the religious-minded must

understand that neither is there any blessing or initiation which, if only we could receive it, nor any mysterious or magical formula or ritual which, if only we could discover it, would enable us to achieve transformation instantly. Comes little by little, just as a building is constructed brick by brick, or, as the Tibetan expression has it, an ocean is formed drop by drop. And, because, unlike our bodies which soon get sick, old and worn out, the afflictive emotions never age. It is important to realize that dealing with them is a life long struggle. Nor should the reader suppose that what we are talking about here is mere acquisition of knowledge. It is not even a question of developing the conviction that may come from such knowledge. What we are talking about is gaining experience of virtue through constant practice and familiarization such that it becomes spontaneous. What we find is that the more we develop concern for others' well-being, the easier it becomes to act in others' interests. As we become habituated to the effort required, so the struggle to sustain it lessens. Eventually it will become second nature. But there are no shortcuts.

Engaging in virtuous activities is a bit like bringing up a young child. A great many factors are involved. And, especially at the beginning, we need to be be prudent and skillful in our endeavours to transform our habits and dispositions. We also need to be realistic about what we can expect to achieve. It took us a long time to become the way we are and habits are not changed overnight.

So whilst it is good to raise our sights as we progress, it is a mistake to judge our behaviour using the ideal as a standard. Just as in college, it would be foolish to judge our child's performance as a first-year student from the perspective of a graduate. Graduation is the ideal, not the standard. For this reason, far more effective than short bursts of heroic effort followed by periods of laxity is to work steadily like a stream flowing towards our goal of transformation.

One method that is very helpful in sustaining us in this life-long task of transformation is to adopt a daily routine which can be adjusted according to our progress. Of course, as with the practise of virtue in general, this is one of the things religious practice encourages. But that is no reason why non-believers should not use some of the ideas and techniques which have served humanity so well over the course of millennia. Making a habit of concern for others' well-being, and spending a few minutes on waking in the morning reflecting on the value of conducting our lives in an ethically disciplined manner is a good way to start the day no matter what our beliefs. The same is true of taking some time at the end of each day to review how successful we have been in this. Such a discipline is very helpful in developing our determination not to behave self-indulgently.

If these suggestions sound somewhat onerous to the reader searching not for *nirvana*, nor for salvation, but merely for ordinary human happiness, it is worth reminding ourselves that what brings us greatest joy and satisfaction in life are those actions we undertake out of concern for others. Indeed, we can go further. Each of the fundamental questions of human existence, such as why we are here, where we are going and whether the phenomenal world had a beginning, elicits different responses in different philosophical traditions. But it is self-evident that a generous heart and wholesome actions lead to greater peace. It is equally clear that their negative counterparts bring undesirable consequences. Happiness arises from virtuous causes. If we truly desire to be happy, there is no other way to proceed but by way of virtue: it is the method by which happiness is achieved. And, we might add, the basis of virtue, its ground, is ethical discipline.

CHAPTER EIGHT

THE ETHICS OF COMPASSION

We noted earlier that all the world's major religions stress the importance of cultivating love and compassion. In the Buddhist philosophical tradition, different levels of attainment are described. At a basic level, compassion (*nying-je*) is understood mainly in terms of empathy – our ability to enter into and, to some extent, share others' suffering. This, Buddhists – and perhaps others – believe, can be developed to the degree that not only does our compassion arise without any effort, but it is unconditional, undifferentiated and universal in scope. A feeling of intimacy towards all other sentient beings, including those who would harm us, is generated. This is likened in the Buddhist literature to the love a mother has for her only child.

But this sense of equanimity towards all others is not seen as an end in itself. Rather it is seen as the spring-board to a still greater love. Because our capacity for empathy is innate, and because the ability to reason is also an innate faculty, compassion shares the characteristics of consciousness itself. The potential we have for it is therefore stable and continuous. It is not a resource, which can be used up – as water is used up when we boil it. Though it can be described in terms of activity, it is not like a physical activity for which we train, like jumping, and which once we reach a certain height we can go no further. On the contrary, when we enhance our sensitivity towards others' suffering through deliberately opening ourselves up to it, it is believed that we can gradually extend our compassion to the point where the individual feels so moved by even the subtlest suffering of others that they come to have an overwhelming sense of responsibility towards those others. This causes the one who is compassionate to dedicate himself or herself entirely to helping others overcome both suffering and the causes of suffering. In Tibetan, this ultimate level of attainment is called *nying-je chenmo*, literally 'great compassion'.

Now I am not suggesting that in order to lead an ethically wholesome life, each individual must attain these advanced states of spiritual development. If we can keep the aspiration to develop *nying-je chenmo*, or great compassion as an ideal, based on the simple recognition that, just as I do so do all others desire to be happy and not to suffer, it will naturally have a significant impact on our outlook. It will serve as a constant reminder against selfishness and partiality. It will remind us that there is little to be gained from being kind and generous because we hope to win something in return. It will remind us that actions motivated by the desire to create a good name for ourselves are still selfish, however much they may appear to be acts of kindness. It will also remind us that there is nothing exceptional about acts of charity towards those we already feel close to. It will help us recognize that the bias we naturally feel towards our families and friends is actually a highly unreliable thing on which to base ethical conduct.

Why is this? Because as long as the individuals in question continue to meet our expectations, all is well. But as soon as they fail to do so, someone we consider a dear friend one day can become our sworn enemy the next. Similarly, if our love for someone is based largely on attraction, whether it be looks or some other superficial characteristic, our feelings for that person are liable, over time, to evaporate. If they lose the quality we found alluring, or we find ourselves no longer satisfied by it, the situation can change completely – this despite it being the same person. Love as we usually find it tends to exaggerate one small quality, causing the person in question to appear to us in an entirely positive light. If that quality changes, or our attitude changes, our love for that person changes. With genuinely compassionate love, on the other hand, neither the other's appearance nor his or her behaviour affect our underlying attitude.

Consider, too, that our feelings towards others habitually depend very much on their circumstances. Most people feel sympathy when they see someone who is handicapped. When they see others who are wealthier, or better educated, or better placed socially they immediately feel envious and competitive towards them. Our negative feelings prevent us from seeing the sameness of ourselves and all others. We forget that just like us, they desire to be happy and not to suffer. The struggle is thus to overcome these feelings of partiality.

Although, certainly, developing genuine compassion for our loved ones is the obvious and appropriate place to start, we need to recognize that there are ultimately no grounds for discriminating against others. We are all in the same position as a doctor confronted by ten patients suffering the same serious illness. Each is equally deserving of treatment. The reader should not suppose that what is being advocated here is a state of detached indifference towards our close ones, however. What is being suggested is that we need to strive for even-handedness in our approach towards all others, a level ground into which we can plant the seed of *nying-je chenmo*, of great love and compassion. The idea behind this is that, in so doing, we can begin to transcend the limitations of our habitual feelings of bias towards those we are close to.

If we can begin to relate to others on the basis of such equanimity, our compassion will not depend on the fact that so and so is my husband, my wife, my relative, my friend. Rather a feeling of closeness towards all others will begin to develop based on the simple recognition that, just like myself, all wish to be happy and to avoid suffering. In other words we will start to relate to others on the basis of our common nature. Again, we can think of this in terms of an ideal, and one which it is immensely difficult to attain. But for myself, I find it one which is profoundly inspiring and helpful.

Let us now consider the role of compassionate love and kind-heartedness in our daily lives. Does the ideal of developing it to the point where it is unconditional mean that we must abandon our own interests entirely? Not at all. In fact, it is the best way of serving them – indeed it could even be said to constitute the wisest course to fulfil our own interests. For if it is correct that qualities such as love, patience, tolerance and forgiveness are those in which happiness consists, and if it is also correct that compassion, as I have defined it, is both the source and the fruit of these qualities, then the more we are compassionate, the more we provide for our own happiness. Thus any idea that concern for others, though a noble quality, is a matter for our private lives only is simply short-sighted. Compassion belongs to every sphere of activity including, of course, the work place.

Here, though, I must acknowledge the existence of a perception – shared by many it seems – that compassion is, if not actually an impediment, at least irrelevant to professional life. Personally, I would argue that not only is it relevant but that when compassion is lacking, our activities are in danger of becoming destructive. This is because when we ignore the question of others' well-being, there is nothing in which to situate restraint of our actions. An ethics of compassion helps provide the necessary foundation of and motivation for both restraint and the cultivation of virtue. When we begin to develop a genuine appreciation of the value of compassion, our outlook on others automatically begins to change. This alone can serve as a powerful influence on the way we conduct our lives. If, for example, the temptation to deceive others arises, our compassion for them would prevent us from entertaining the idea. And if we realized that our work itself was in danger of being exploited to the detriment of others, it would cause us to disengage from it. Take an imaginary case of a scientist whose research seemed likely to be a source of suffering. He or she would recognize this and act accordingly, even if this meant abandoning the project.

I do not deny that genuine problems can arise when we dedicate ourselves to the ideal of compassion. In the case of a scientist who feels unable to continue in the direction his or her work is going, this could have profound consequences for themselves and their families. Likewise, those engaged in the caring professions – in medicine, counselling and social work and so on – or even those looking after someone at home may sometimes become so exhausted by their duties that they begin to feel overwhelmed. Constant exposure to suffering, coupled occasionally with a feeling of being taken for granted can induce feelings of helplessness and even despair. Or it can happen that individuals may find themselves performing outwardly generous actions just for the sake of it – simply going through the motions as it were. When left unchecked, this can lead to insensitivity towards others' suffering. If this starts to happen, it is best to disengage for a short while and make a deliberate effort to re-awaken one's sensitivity. This can be done by reflecting on the fact that despair is never a solution. It is rather the ultimate failure. Therefore, as the Tibetan expression has it, even if the rope breaks nine times, we must splice back together a tenth time. In this way, even if ultimately we do fail, at least there will be no feelings of regret. If we combine this insight with a clear appreciation of our potential to benefit others, we find that we can begin to restore our hope and confidence.

Some people may object to this ideal on the grounds that, by entering into others' suffering, we bring suffering on ourselves. To an extent this is true. But I suggest that there is an important qualitative distinction to be made between experiencing one's own suffering and experiencing suffering in the course of sharing in others'. In the case of one's own suffering, given that it is involuntary, there is a sense of oppression: it seems to come from outside us. By contrast, sharing in someone else's suffering must at some level involve a degree of voluntariness which itself is indicative of a certain inner strength. For this reason, the disturbance it may cause is considerably less likely to paralyse us than our own suffering.

Of course, even as an ideal, the notion of developing unconditional compassion is daunting. Most people, including myself, must struggle to reach the point at which putting others' interests on a par with our own becomes easy. We should not allow this to put us off, however. Undoubtedly there will be obstacles on the way to developing a genuinely warm heart, there is the deep consolation of knowing that in doing so we are creating the conditions for our own happiness. As I mentioned earlier, the more we truly desire to benefit others, the greater the strength and confidence we develop and the greater the peace and happiness we experience. If this still seems unlikely, it is worth asking ourselves how else we are to do so? With violence and aggression? Of course not. With money? Perhaps up to a point, but no further. But with love, by sharing in others' suffering, by recognizing ourselves clearly in all others – especially those who are disadvantaged and those whose rights are not respected

– and by helping them to be happy. Through love, through kindness, through compassion we establish understanding between ourselves and others. This is how we forge unity and harmony.

Compassion and love are not mere luxuries. As the source both of inner and external peace, they are fundamental to the continued survival of our species. On the one hand, they constitute non-violence in action. On the other they are the source of all spiritual qualities: of forgiveness, tolerance and all the virtues. Moreover they are the very thing that gives meaning to our activities and makes them constructive. There is nothing amazing about being highly educated; there is nothing amazing about being rich. Only if the individual has a warm heart do these attributes become worthwhile.

So to those who say that the Dalai Lama is being unrealistic in advocating this ideal of unconditional love, I urge them to experiment with it nonetheless. They will discover that when we reach beyond the confines of narrow self-interest, our hearts become filled with strength. Peace and joy become our constant companion. It breaks down barriers of every kind and in the end destroys the notion of my interest as separate from others' interest. But most importantly, insofar as ethics is concerned, where love of one's neighbour, affection, kindness and compassion live, we find that ethical conduct is automatic. Ethically wholesome actions arise naturally in the context of compassion.

CHAPTER NINE

ETHICS AND SUFFERING

I have suggested that we all desire happiness, that genuine happiness is characterized by peace, that peace is most surely attained when our actions are motivated by concern for others and that this, in turn, entails ethical discipline and dealing positively with afflictive emotion. I have also suggested that in our quest for happiness we naturally and properly seek to avoid suffering. Let us now examine this quality, or state, we wish so strongly to be free from but which lies at the very heart of our existence.

Suffering and pain are inalienable facts of life. A sentient being, according to my usual definition, is one which

ANCIENT WISDOM, MODERN WORLD

has the capacity to feel pain and suffer. One could also say that it is our experience of suffering which connects us to others. It is the basis of our capacity for empathy. But beyond this, we can observe that suffering falls into two interrelated categories. There are the 'avoidable' forms which arise as a consequence of such phenomena as war, poverty, violence, crime – and even things such as illiteracy and certain diseases. Then there are the 'unavoidable' forms – which include such phenomena as sickness, old age and death. So far, we have been speaking about dealing with avoidable, human-created-suffering. Now I want to look more closely at that which is unavoidable.

The problems and difficulties we face in life are not at all like famine or drought. We cannot protect ourselves from them merely by taking suitable precautions, such as storing food. In the case of sickness, for example, no matter how fit we keep ourselves, or how carefully we regulate our diet, eventually our bodies give in to physical problems. And when they do, the impact on our lives can be serious: we may be prevented from doing the things we want to do and from going to the places we want to go. Often we are prevented from eating the foods we like. Instead we have to take medicines which taste awful. If things get really bad, we can find ourselves enduring days and nights wracked with pain and we may long to die.

So far as ageing is concerned, from the day we are born, we are faced with the prospect of growing old and losing the suppleness of youth. In time, our hair falls out, our teeth fall out, we lose our eyesight and our hearing. We can no longer digest the foods we once enjoyed. Eventually we find that we cannot recall events which once were so vivid, or even remember the names of those closest to us. Should we live long enough, we will reach such a state of decrepitude that others may find the mere sight of us repulsive, though this is precisely the time we will have most need of them.

Then death comes – almost a taboo subject in modern society it seems. This also entails suffering, though eventually we may look forward to it as a relief. Regardless of what may come afterwards, death means that we are parted from our loved ones, from our precious belongings, indeed from the very body which has been our constant companion in life.

To this brief description of unavoidable suffering we must, however, add another category: the suffering entailed in meeting with the unwanted – of mishaps and accidents. There is also the suffering of having what we want taken away from us, as we refugees have lost our countries, many forcibly parted from their loved ones. There is the suffering caused by not obtaining what we desire though we may put great effort into doing so. Despite breaking our back working in the fields, the harvest fails. Despite working night and day at a business venture, it is not successful, though through no fault of our own. Then there is the suffering of uncertainty, of never knowing when and where we will meet with adversity. From our own experience, we all know how this can lead to feelings of insecurity and anxiety, and this undermines everything we do. There is also the suffering of lack of contentment which arises even when we achieve all that we have striven for. Such events are part of our everyday experience as human beings who desire happiness and wish not to suffer.

As if this were not enough, there is the fact that the very experiences which ordinarily we suppose will be pleasurable turn out to be a source of suffering themselves. They seem to offer fulfilment but they do not actually provide it – a phenomenon we looked at earlier in the discussion on happiness. In fact, if we think carefully, we will find that we perceive such experiences as pleasurable only insofar as they offset more explicit suffering, as when, for example, we eat to assuage hunger. We take one mouthful, then two, three, four, five, and enjoy the experience. But quite soon we begin to find eating objectionable. If we do not stop, eventually it will harm us – just as nearly every worldly pleasure comes to harms us when carried to an extreme. This is why contentment is indispensable if we are to be genuinely happy.

All these manifestations of suffering are essentially unavoidable and are indeed natural facts of existence. This does not mean that, finally, there is nothing we can do about them. Nor do I mean to suggest that it is unrelated to the question of ethical discipline. It is true that, according to Buddhist and other Indian religious philosophies, suffering is seen as a consequence of *karma*.

To suppose, as do quite a lot of people, Easterners and Westerners alike it seems, that this means that everything we experience is predetermined is totally wrong, however. Still less is it an excuse not to take responsibility in whatever situation we find ourselves.

Since the term *karma* appears to have entered everyday vocabulary, it might be worthwhile to clarify the concept somewhat. *Karma* is a Sanskrit word meaning action. It denotes an active force, the inference being that the outcome of future events can be influenced by our actions. To suppose that *karma* is some sort of independent energy which predestines the course of our whole life is simply incorrect. Who creates *karma*? We ourselves, by what we think, say, do, desire, and omit, create *karma*. As I write, for example, the very action creates new circumstances and causes other events. My words cause a response in the reader's mind. In everything we do, there is cause and effect, cause and effect. In our daily lives, the food we eat, the work we undertake, our relaxation, all these things are a function of action: our action. This is *karma*. We cannot therefore throw up our hands whenever we find ourselves confronted by unavoidable suffering. To say that every misfortune is simply the result of *karma* is tantamount to saying that we are totally powerless in life. If this were correct, there would be no cause for hope. We might as well pray for the end of the world.

A proper appreciation of cause and effect suggests that far from being powerless, there is much we can do about how we experience suffering. Old age, sickness and death are inevitable. But as with the torments of negative thoughts and emotions, we certainly have a choice in terms of how we respond to the occurrence of suffering. If we wish, we can adopt a more dispassionate and rational approach and on that basis we can discipline our response to it. On the other hand, we can simply fret about our misfortunes. But when we do, we become frustrated. As a result, afflictive emotions arise and our peace of mind is destroyed. When we do not restrain our tendency to respond negatively to suffering it becomes a source of negative thoughts and emotions. There is thus a clear relationship between the impact suffering has on our heart and mind and our practise of inner discipline.

Our basic attitude towards suffering makes a great difference to the way in which we experience it. Imagine, for example, two people suffering an identical form of terminal cancer. The only difference between these two patients is their outlook on it. One sees it as something to be accepted and if possible transformed into an opportunity for developing inner strength. The other responds to his or her circumstances with fear, bitterness and anxiety about the future. Now although on the physical level, there is no difference between the two of them in terms of what they are suffering, in actual fact there is a profound difference in their experience of it. In the case of the latter, in addition to the physical suffering itself, there is the added pain of inner suffering.

This suggests that the degree to which suffering affects us is largely up to us. It is therefore essential to keep a proper perspective on our experience of suffering. When we look at a particular problem from close up, it tends to fill our whole field of vision and look enormous. If, however, we look at the same problem from a distance, automatically we will start to see it in relation to other things. This simple act makes a tremendous difference. It enables us to see that, though a given situation may truly be tragic, even the most unfortunate event has innumerable aspects and can be approached from many different angles. Indeed, it is very rare, if not impossible, to find a situation which is negative no matter how we look at it.

When tragedy or misfortune come our way, as surely they must, it can be very helpful to make a comparison with another event, or to call to mind a similar or worse situation that has befallen, if not ourselves, then others before us. If we can actually shift our focus away from self and towards others, we experience a freeing effect. It seems there is something about the dynamics of self-absorption which tends to magnify the suffering of the one who is in that state. If we come to see our suffering in relation to that of others, we begin to recognize that, relatively speaking, it is not all that significant. This enables us to maintain our peace of mind much more easily than if we concentrate on our problems to the exclusion of all else.

So far as my own experience is concerned, I find that when, for example, I hear bad news from Tibet – and sadly this is quite often – naturally my immediate response is one of great sadness. However, by placing it in context and by reminding myself that – given the basic human disposition towards affection – freedom, truth and justice must eventually prevail, I find I can cope reasonably well. Feelings of helpless anger, which do nothing but poison the mind, embitter the heart and enfeeble the will seldom arise, even following the worst news.

It is also worth remembering that the time of greatest gain in terms of wisdom and inner strength is often that of greatest difficulty. With the right approach – and here we see once more the supreme importance of developing a positive attitude – the experience of suffering can open our eyes to reality. For example, my own experience of life as a refugee has helped me realize that the formality, which was such an important part of my life in Tibet, was quite unnecessary. We also find that our confidence and self-reliance can grow and our courage become strengthened as a result of suffering. This can be inferred from what we see in the world around us. Within our own refugee community, for example, amongst the survivors of our early years in exile are a number who, though they suffered terribly, are amongst the strongest spiritually – and the most cheerfully carefree – individuals I have the privilege to know. Conversely, we find that in the face of even relatively slight adversity, some people who have everything are inclined to lose hope and become despondent. There is a natural tendency for wealth to spoil us. The result is that we find it progressively more difficult to bear easily the problems everyone must encounter from time to time.

Let us now consider what options are open to us when we actually encounter a particular problem. At one extreme, we can allow ourselves to be overwhelmed. At the other, we can simply go on a picnic or take a holiday and ignore it. The third possibility is to face up to the situation directly. This involves examining it, analysing it, determining its causes and finding out how to deal with them.

Though this third course may occasion us additional pain in the short term, it is clearly preferable to the other two courses of action. If we try to avoid or deny a given problem by simply ignoring it or taking to drink or drugs – or even some forms of meditation or prayer as a means of escape – while there is a chance of short-term relief, the problem itself remains. Such an approach is simply avoiding the issue, not resolving it. Once again, the danger is that, in addition to the initial problem, there follows mental and emotional unrest. The afflictions of anxiety, fear and doubt build up. Eventually, this can lead to anger and despair, with all the further potential for suffering for ourselves and others which it entails.

Imagine being shot in the stomach. The pain is excruciating. What are we to do? Of course, we need to have the bullet removed and we undergo surgery. This adds to the trauma. Yet we gladly accept this in order to overcome the original problem. Similarly, due to infection, or to catastrophic damage, it may be necessary to lose a limb in order to save our life. But again, naturally, we are prepared to accept this lesser form of suffering if it will spare us the greater suffering of death. It is only common sense to undergo hardship voluntarily when we see that by doing so we are able to avoid worse. Saying this, I admit that this is not always an easy judgement to make. When I was around six or seven years of age, I was inoculated against smallpox. Had I realized how much it would hurt, I doubt whether I could have been persuaded that vaccination constituted a lesser suffering than the disease itself. The pain lasted fully ten days and I still have four large scars as a result!

If the prospect of confronting our suffering head-on can sometimes seem a bit daunting, it is very helpful to remember that nothing within the realm of what we commonly experience is permanent. All phenomena are subject to change and decay. Secondly, the interdependent nature of reality means that we are mistaken if we ever suppose that our experience of suffering – or happiness for that matter – can be attributed to a single source. As we saw earlier, everything that is arises within the context of innumerable causes and conditions. If this were not so, as soon as we came into contact with something that we considered good, we would automatically become happy.

Whenever we encountered something we considered bad, we would automatically become sad. The causes of joy and sorrow would be easy to identify and life would be very simple. We would have good reason to become attached to one sort of person or thing or event and to be angry with and want to avoid others. But that is not the case. No single phenomena is either wholly desirable or wholly objectionable.

Personally I find the advice given in respect of suffering by the great Indian scholar-saint, Shantideva enormously helpful. It is essential, he said, that when we face difficulties of whatever sort not to let them paralyse us. If we do, we are in danger of being totally overwhelmed by them. Instead, using our critical faculties, we should examine the nature of the problem itself. If we find it is such that there exists the possibility we could solve it by some means or other, there is no need for anxiety. The rational thing would then be to devote all one's energy to finding that means and acting on it. If, on the other hand, we find that the nature of the problem is such that there simply can be no solution, there is no point worrying about it. If nothing can change the situation, worrying only makes it worse. Taken out of the context of the philosophical text in which it appears as the culmination of a complex series of reflections, Shantideva's approach may sound somewhat simplistic. But its very beauty lies in this quality of simplicity. And no one could argue with its sheer common sense.

As to the possibility that suffering has some actual purpose, we will not go into that here. But to the extent that our experience of suffering reminds us of what all others also endure, it serves as a powerful injunction to practise compassion and refrain from causing others pain. And to the extent that, suffering awakens our empathy and causes us to connect with others, it can serve as the basis of compassion and love. Here I am reminded of the example of another great Tibetan scholar and religious practitioner who spent more than twenty years in prison enduring the most terrible treatment including torture, following the occupation of our country. During that time, those students of his who had escaped into exile would often tell me that the letters he wrote and had smuggled out of jail, contained the most profound teachings on love and compassion they had ever encountered. Unfortunate events, though potentially a source of anger and despair, have equal potential to be a source of spiritual growth. Whether or not this is the outcome depends on our response.

CHAPTER TEN

THE NEED FOR DISCERNMENT

In our survey of ethics and spiritual development, we have spoken a great deal about the need for discipline. This may seem somewhat old-fashioned, even implausible in an age and culture where so much emphasis is placed on the goal of self-fulfilment. But the reason for peoples' negative view of discipline is, I suggest, mainly due to what is generally understood by the term. People tend to associate it with something imposed against their will. It is worth repeating, therefore, that what we are talking about when we speak of ethical discipline is something that we adopt voluntarily on the basis of full recognition of its benefits. This is not an alien concept. We do not hesitate to accept discipline when it comes to our physical health. On doctors' advice, we avoid foods that are harmful even when we crave them. Instead we eat those that benefit us. And whilst it is true that, at the initial stage, self-discipline, even when voluntarily adopted, may involve hardship and even a degree of struggle, through habituation and diligent application, this lessens over time. It is a bit like diverting the course of a stream. First we have to dig the channel and build up its banks. Then, when the water is released into it, we may have to make adjustments here and there. But when the course is fully established, it flows freely.

Ethical discipline is indispensable because it is the means by which we mediate between the competing claims of my right to happiness and all others' equal right. Naturally, there will always be those who suppose their own happiness to be of such importance that others' pain is of no consequence. But this is short-sighted. No one truly benefits from causing harm to others. Whatever immediate advantage is gained at the expense of someone else is necessarily only temporary. In the long run, causing others hurt and disturbing their peace and happiness causes us anxiety. Because our actions have an impact both on ourselves and others, when we lack discipline, eventually anxiety arises in our mind and deep in our heart we come to feel a sense of disquiet. Conversely, whatever hardship it entails, disciplining our response to negative thoughts and emotions will be found to cause us fewer problems in the long run than indulging in acts of selfishness.

Nevertheless, it is worth saying again that ethical discipline entails more than just restraint. It also entails the cultivation of virtue. Love and compassion, patience, tolerance and forgiveness are essential qualities. When they are present in our lives, everything we do becomes an instrument to benefit the whole human family. Even in terms of our daily occupation – whether this is looking after children in the home, working in a factory, or serving the community as a doctor, lawyer, business person, or teacher – our actions contribute towards the well-being of all. And because ethical discipline is what facilitates these, the very qualities which give meaning and value to our existence, it is clearly something to be embraced with enthusiasm and conscious effort.

Before looking at how we apply this inner discipline in our interactions with others, it may be worth reviewing the grounds for defining ethical conduct in terms of non-harming. As we have seen, given the complex nature of reality, it is very difficult to say that a particular act or type of act is right or wrong in itself. Ethical conduct is thus not something we engage in because it is somehow right in itself. We do so because we recognize that, just as I desire to be happy and to avoid suffering, so do all others. For this reason, a meaningful ethical system divorced from the question of an individual's experience of suffering and happiness is hard to envisage.

Of course, if we want to ask all sorts of difficult questions based on metaphysics, ethical discourse can become exceedingly complicated. Yet whilst it is true that ethical practice cannot be reduced to a mere exercise in logic, whichever way we look at it, in the end we are brought back to the fundamental questions of happiness and suffering. Why is happiness good and suffering bad for us? Perhaps there is no conclusive answer. But we can observe that it is in our nature to prefer the one to the other, just as it is to prefer the better over that which is merely good. We simply aspire to happiness and not to suffering. If we were to go further and ask why this is so, surely the ultimate answer would have to be something like: That's the way it is, or, God made us this way.

So far as the ethical character of a given action is concerned, we have seen how this is dependant on a great many factors. Time and circumstance have an important bearing on the matter. But so too does the element of freedom or lack of it enjoyed by the individual. A negative act can be considered more serious when the perpetrator commits the deed with full freedom as opposed to someone who is acting against his or her will. Similarly, given the lack of remorse this reflects, negative acts repeatedly indulged can be considered graver than an isolated act. But we must also consider the intention behind the action, as well as its content. The overriding question, however, concerns the individual's spiritual state, their overall state of heart and mind (*kun-long*) in the moment of action. Because, generally speaking, this is the area over which we have most control, it is the most significant element in determining the ethical character of our acts. As we have seen, when our intentions are polluted by selfishness, by hatred, or by desire to deceive, however much our acts may have the appearance of being constructive, inevitably their impact will be negative, both for self and others.

How, though, are we to apply this principle of non-harming when confronted with an ethical dilemma? This is where our critical and imaginative powers come in. These I have described in terms of our most precious resource, one of the things that distinguish us from animals. We have seen how afflictive emotions destroys them. And we have seen how important they are in learning to deal with suffering. Insofar as these faculties are concerned, they are what enable us to discriminate between temporary and long-term benefit, to determine the degree of ethical fitness of the different course of action open to us, to assess the likely outcome of our actions and thereby to set aside lesser goals in order to achieve greater ones. In the case of a dilemma, we need therefore in the first instance to consider the particularity of the situation in the light of what, in the Buddhist tradition, is called the 'union of skilful means and insight'. Here 'skilful means' can be understood in terms of the efforts we make to ensure that our deeds are motivated by compassion. 'Insight' refers to our critical faculties and how, in response to the different factors involved, we adjust the ideal of non-harming to the context of the situation. We could call it the faculty of wise discernment.

Employing this faculty – which is especially important where there is no appeal to religious belief – involves constantly checking our outlook and asking ourselves whether we are being broad-minded or narrow-minded? Have we taken into account the overall situation or are we considering only specifics? Is our view short-term or long-term? Are we being short-sighted or clear-eyed? Is our motive genuinely compassionate when considered in relation to the totality of all beings. Or is our compassion limited just to our families, our friends and those we identify with closely? Just as in the practice of mindfulness in which we focus on our thoughts and emotions, we need to think, think, think.

Of course, it will not always be possible to devote time to careful discernment. Sometimes we have to act at once. This is why our spiritual development is of such critical importance in ensuring that our actions are ethically sound. The more spontaneous our actions, the more they are likely to reflect our inner disposition in that moment. If this is unwholesome, our acts are bound to be destructive. For this reason, it is useful to have a set of basic ethical precepts, which we can be apply in our daily lives. However, in adopting such precepts, it is best when we think of them less in terms of moral legislation than as injunctions always to keep others' interests at heart and in the forefront of our minds.

So far as the content of such precepts is concerned, it is doubtful whether we could do better than turn to the basic ethical directives articulated not only by each of the world's great religions but also by the greater part of the humanist philosophical tradition. The consensus amongst them, despite differences of opinion concerning grounds, is compelling to my mind. All are agreed on the negativity of killing, stealing, telling lies, of sexual misconduct, and of speaking with malicious intent. In addition, from the point of view of motivational factors, all agree on the need to avoid hatred, pride, covetousness, envy, greed, lust, destructive ideology and so on.

Some people may wonder whether the injunctions against sexual misconduct are really necessary in these times of simple and effective contraception. But to see why, consider, for example, a case of infidelity. Firstly, given that wholesome ethical conduct entails considering the impact of our actions not only on ourselves but on others too, there are the feelings of third parties to consider. Even if our actions remain undiscovered, it is highly likely that our subsequent behaviour will arouse suspicion and fear in our partner, thereby destroying his or her peace of mind. Then there is the question of the lasting impact that upset in the family can have on our children. It is now more or less universally accepted that they are the principal victims both of family break-up and of unhealthy relationships in the home. Also from our own perspective as the person who has commited the act, we must acknowledge that it is likely to have the negative effect of gradually corroding our self-respect. Finally, infidelity may cause other gravely negative acts to result as a direct consequence – lying and deception being perhaps the least of them. An unwanted pregnancy could easily be the cause of a desperate prospective parent seeking an abortion.

If we think in this way, it becomes obvious that the momentary pleasures afforded by unfaithfulness are far outweighed by the risk of the grave negative consequences for ourselves and others. Rather than seeing strictures against sexual misconduct as a limit to freedom, we do better to see them as common sense reminders that such actions can undermine our well-being and that of others.

Does this mean that following precepts takes precedent over wise discernment? No. Ethically sound conduct depends on us applying the principle of non-harming. However, there are bound to be situations where any course of action would appear to involve breaking a precept. Under such circumstances, we must use our intelligence to judge which course of action will be least harmful in the long run. Imagine, for example, a situation in which we witness someone running away from a group of people armed with knives and clearly intent on doing harm. We see the fugitive disappear into a doorway. Moments later, one of the pursuers comes up to us and asks which way he or she went? Now on the one hand, we do not want to lie, to injure the other's trust. On the other, if we tell the truth, we realize that we may contribute to the injury or death of a fellow human being. Whatever we decide, the appropriate course of action would appear to involve a negative deed. Under such circumstances, because we are certain that in so doing we are serving a higher purpose – preserving someone from harm – it might well be appropriate to say, 'Oh I didn't see him' or vaguely, 'I think he went the other way'. We have to take into account the overall situation and weigh the benefits of telling a lie and telling the truth and do that which we judge to be least harmful overall. In other words, the moral value of a given act is to be judged in relation to time, place and circumstance and to the interests of the totality of all others in the future as well as the present. We must remember whilst a given act may be ethically sound under one particular set of circumstances, the same act at another time and place and under a different set of circumstances may not be.

What though are we to do when it comes to others? What are we to do when they seem clearly to be engaging in actions which we consider wrong? The first thing is to remember that unless we know down to the last detail the full range of circumstances, both internal and external, we can never be sufficiently clear about individual situations to be able to pronounce with complete certainty on the morality of another's actions. Of course, there will be extreme situations when the negative character of another's acts will be self-evident. But mostly this is not the case. This is why it is far more useful to be aware of a single shortcoming in ourselves than it is to be aware of thousand in somebody else. If the fault is our own, we are in a position to correct it.

Nevertheless, recognizing that there is an essential distinction to be made between a person and their behaviour, we may come across circumstances in which it is appropriate to take action. In everyday life, it is normal and fitting to adapt in some degree to one's friends and acquaintances and to respect their wishes. The ability to do so is considered a good quality. But when we mix with those who clearly indulge in negative behaviour, seeking only their own benefit and ignoring others, we risk losing our own sense of direction. As a result, our ability to help others becomes endangered. There is a Tibetan proverb which says: when we lie on a mountain of gold, some of it rubs off on us; the same happens if we lie on a mountain of dirt. We are right to avoid such people, though we must be careful not to cut them off completely. Indeed, there are sure to be times when it is appropriate to try to stop them acting in this way – provided of course that our motives in doing so are pure and our methods are non-harming. Again, the key principles are compassion and insight.

The same is true in respect of the ethical dilemmas

we face at the level of society, especially the difficult and challenging questions posed by modern science and technology. For example, in the field of medicine, it has become possible to prolong life in cases which would have been hopeless just a few years ago. This can of course be a source of great joy. But quite often, complicated and very delicate questions arise concerning the limits of care. I think that there can be no general rule in respect of this. There is likely to be a multiplicity of competing considerations, which we must assess in the light of reason and compassion. If it becomes necessary to take a difficult decision on behalf of a patient, we must take into account all the various elements. These will of course be different in each case. For example, if we prolong the life of a person who is critically ill but whose mind remains lucid, we give that person the opportunity to think and feel in a way that only a human being can. On the other hand, we must consider whether in doing so they will experience great physical and mental suffering as a result of extreme measures taken to keep them alive. This in itself is not an over-riding factor, however. As someone who believes in the continuation of consciousness after the death of the body, I would argue that it is much better to have pain with this human body. At least we can benefit from the care of others' whereas, if we choose to die, we may find that we have to endure suffering in some other form.

If the patient is not conscious and is therefore unable

to participate in the decision making process, this is yet another problem. And on top of everything, there are the wishes of the family to take into account, along with the immense problems that prolonged care can cause them and others. For example it may be that in order to continue to support one life, valuable funds are kept from projects which would benefit many others. If there is a general principle, I think it is simply that we recognize the supreme preciousness of life and try to ensure that when the time comes, the dying person departs quietly and as serenely and peacefully as possible.

In the case of work in such fields as those of genetics and biotechnology, because lives may be at stake, the principle of non-harming takes on special importance. If the motivation behind such research is merely profit, or fame, or if research is carried out just for its own sake, only narrow interests are served. I am thinking particularly of the development of techniques to manipulate things like physical attributes, such as gender, or even hair and eye colour, which can be used commercially to exploit the prejudices of parents. Indeed, let me say here that whilst it is difficult to be categorically against all forms of genetic experimentation, this is such a delicate area that it is essential that all those involved proceed with caution and deep humility. They must be especially aware of the potential for abuse. It is vital that they keep in mind the wider implications of what they are doing and, most importantly, ensure that their motives are genuinely compassionate. For if the general principle behind such work is simply utility, whereby what is deemed useless can legitimately be used to benefit what is judged to be useful, there is nothing to stop us from subordinating the rights of those who fall into the former category to those who fall into the latter. The attribute of utility can never justify the deprivation of an individual's rights, this is a highly dangerous and very slippery slope.

Recently I saw a BBC television documentary about cloning. Using computer generated imagery, this film showed a creature some scientists were working on, a sort of semi-human being with large eyes and several other recognizably human features lying down in a cage. Of course at present this is just fantasy but, they explained, it is possible to foresee a time when it will be possible to create beings like this. They could then be bred and their organs and other parts of their anatomy used as 'spare parts' in surgery for the benefit of human beings. I was utterly appalled at this. Oh terrible, the idea that one day we might actually create sentient beings specifically for this purpose is sickening. I felt the same at this prospect as I do at the idea of experiments involving human foetuses. Surely this is taking scientific endeavour to an extreme?

At the same time, it is difficult to see how this kind of thing can be prevented. Yes we can promulgate laws. Yes we can have international codes of conduct, and indeed we should have both these. Yet if the individual scientists do not have any sense that what they are doing is grotesque, destructive, and negative in the extreme, then there is no real prospect of putting an end to such disturbing endeavours.

What about issues like vivisection where routinely animals are caused terrible suffering before being killed as a means to furthering scientific knowledge? To a Buddhist, such practices are equally shocking. I can only hope that the rapid advances being made in computer technology will mean there is less and less call for animal experimentation in scientific research. One positive development within modern society is the way in which, together with a growing appreciation of the importance of human rights, people are coming to have greater concern for animals. For example, there is growing recognition of the inhumanity of factory farming. It seems too that more and more people are taking an interest in vegetarianism and cutting down on their consumption of meat. I welcome this. My hope is that in future, this concern will be extended to consideration of even the smallest creatures of the sea.

Here, though, I should perhaps sound a word of warning. The campaigns to protect human and animal life are noble causes. But it is essential that we do not allow ourselves to be carried away by our sense of injustice such that we ignore others' rights. We need to ensure that we are wisely discerning in pursuit of our ideals. And it is vital we recognize that exercising our critical faculties in the ethical realm entails taking responsibility both for our acts and for their underlying motives.

PART THREE

Ethics and Society

CHAPTER ELEVEN

UNIVERSAL RESPONSIBILITY

Our every act has a universal dimension. Because of this, ethical discipline, wholesome conduct and careful discernment are crucial ingredients for a meaningful, happy life. Let us now consider this proposition in relation to the wider community. In the past, families and small communities could exist more or less independently of one another. If they took into account their neighbour's well-being, so much the better. Yet they could survive quite well without this kind of perspective. This is no longer the case. Today's reality is so complex and, so clearly interconnected on the material level that a different outlook is needed. Modern economics is a case in point. A stock market crash on one side of the globe can have a direct effect on the economies of countries on the other. Similarly, our technological achievements are now such that our activities have an unambiguous effect on the natural environment. And the very size of our population means that we cannot afford to ignore others' interests any longer. Indeed, we find that these are often so intertwined that serving our own interests benefits others, even though this may not be our explicit intention. For example, where two families share a single water source, ensuring that it is not polluted benefits both.

Given today's reality, it is therefore essential to cultivate a sense of what I call universal responsibility. This may not be an exact translation of the Tibetan term I have in mind, *chi-sem*, which means literally universal (*chi*) consciousness (*sem*). Although the notion of responsibility is implied rather than explicit in the Tibetan, it is definitely there. When I say that on the basis of concern for others' well-being we can, and should, develop a sense of universal responsibility, I do not, however, mean to suggest that each individual has a direct responsibility for the existence of, for example, wars and famines in different parts of the world. It is true that in Buddhist practice we constantly remind ourselves of our duty to serve all sentient beings in every universe. Similarly, the theist recognizes that devotion to God includes devotion to the welfare of all His creatures. But clearly certain things, such as the poverty of a single village ten thousand miles away, are completely beyond the scope of the individual. What is entailed therefore is not an admission of guilt but, a re-orientation of our heart and mind away from self and towards others. To develop a sense of universal responsibility – of the universal dimension of our every act and of the equal right of all others to happiness and not to suffer – is to develop an attitude of mind whereby, if we see an opportunity to benefit others, then we will take it in preference to merely looking after our own narrow interests. And although we care about what is beyond our scope, we accept it as part of nature and concern ourselves with doing what we can.

An important benefit of developing such a sense of universal responsibility is that it helps us become sensitive to all others – not just those closest to us. We come to see the need to care especially for those members of the human family who suffer most. We recognize the need to avoid causing divisiveness amongst our fellow human beings. And we become aware of the overwhelming importance of contentment.

When we neglect others' well-being and ignore the universal dimension of our actions, it is inevitable we will come to see our interests as separate from theirs. We will overlook the fundamental oneness of the human family. Of course, it is easy to point to numerous factors which work against this notion of unity. These include differences of religious faith, of language, customs, culture and so on. But when we put too much emphasis on superficial differences, and on account of them make small rigid discriminations, we cannot avoid bringing about additional suffering both for ourselves and others. This makes no sense. We humans already have enough problems. We all face death, old age and sickness too – not to mention the inevitability of meeting with disappointment. These we simply cannot avoid. Is this not enough? What is the point of creating still more unnecessary problems simply on the basis of different ways of thinking, or different skin colour?

Judging these realities, we see that both ethics and necessity call for the same response. In order to overcome our tendency to ignore others' needs and rights, we must continually remind ourselves of what is obvious: that basically we are all the same. I come from Tibet. Most of the readers of this book will not be Tibetans. If I were to meet each reader individually and look them over, I would see that the majority do indeed have characteristics superficially different from mine. If I were then to concentrate on these differences, I could certainly amplify them and make them into something important. The result would be that we grow more distant rather than closer. If on the other hand I were to look on each as one of my own kind – as a human being like myself with one nose, two eyes and so forth, ignoring differences of shape and colour, then automatically that sense of distance would fade. I would see that we have the same human flesh and moreover, that just as I want to be happy and to avoid suffering, so do they. On the basis of this recognition, I will quite naturally feel well disposed towards them. And concern for their well-being will arise almost by itself.

Yet it seems to me that whilst most people are willing to accept the need for unity within their own group and, within this, the need to consider others' welfare, the tendency is to neglect the rest of humanity. In doing so, we ignore not only the interdependent nature of reality, but the reality of our situation. If it were possible for one group, or one race, or one nation to gain complete satisfaction and fulfilment by remaining totally independent and self-sufficient within the confines of their own society, then perhaps it could be argued that discrimination against outsiders is justifiable. But this is not the case. In fact, the modern world is such that the interests of a particular community can no longer be considered to lie within the confines of its own boundaries. The cultivation of contentment is crucial to maintaining peaceful coexistence. Discontent breeds acquisitiveness and can never be satisfied.

Paradoxically, if what the individual seeks is by nature infinite, such as the quality of tolerance, contentment is not in question. The more we enhance our ability to be tolerant, the more tolerant we will become. In respect of spiritual qualities, contentment is neither necessary nor desirable. But if what we seek is finite, there is every danger that having acquired it, we will still not be satisfied. In the case of the desire for wealth, even if a person were somehow able to take over the economy of an entire country, there is every chance they would begin to think in terms of acquiring that of other countries too. Desire for what is finite can never really be sated. On the other hand, when we develop contentment, we can never be disappointed or disillusioned when we achieve our aim.

Lack of contentment – or greed – sows the seed of envy and aggressive competitiveness, and leads to a culture of excessive consumerism. The negative atmosphere this creates becomes the context of all kinds of social ills which bring suffering to all members of that community. If it were the case that greed and envy had no side effects whatever, arguably this would be a matter for that community alone. But again this is not the case. In particular, lack of contentment is the source of damage to our natural surroundings and, thereby, of harm to others. Which others? In particular the poor and the weak. Although the rich may be able to move house to avoid, for example, high levels of pollution, within their own community the poor have no choice. Similarly, the people of the poorer nations which do not have the resources to cope with the effects of the richer nations' excesses also suffer. The coming generations will suffer too. And eventually we ourselves will suffer. How? We have to live in the world we are helping to create. If we choose not to modify our behaviour out of respect for others' equal rights to happiness and not to suffer, it will not be long before we begin to notice the negative consequences. Imagine the pollution of an extra two billion cars, for example. It would affect us all. Contentment is not merely an ethical matter. If we do not wish to add to our own experience of suffering, it is a matter of necessity.

For this reason, the culture that demands economic growth every year needs to be modified. Again, this is less a matter of the gap between North and South, between developed and underdeveloped, between rich and poor, being immoral and wrong. It is in some ways more significant is the fact that such inequality is the source of innumerable problems for us all. If it were the case, for example, that Europe was the whole world, rather than home to less than ten per cent of the world's population, the prevailing ideology of endless growth might be justifiable. Yet the world is more than just Europe. The fact is that elsewhere people are starving. Where there are imbalances as profound as these, there are bound to be negative consequences for all, even if they are not equally direct: the rich also feel the symptoms of poverty in their daily lives. Consider, in his context, how the sight of surveillance cameras, and of iron security bars over our windows, actually detracts a little from our sense of security.

As well as awareness of the necessity for contentment, a sense of universal responsibility also leads us to the idea of commitment to truth. What is truth? We can think of the nature of truth and untruth in terms of the relationship between appearance and reality. Sometimes these synchronize, often they do not. But when they do, that is truth as I understand it. So truth exists when our actions are what they seem to be. When we pretend to be one thing but in reality we are something else, suspicion develops in others, causing fear. And fear is something we all wish to avoid. Conversely, when in our interactions with our neighbours we are open and sincere in everything we say and think and do, people have no need to fear us. This holds true both for the individual and for communities. Moreover, when we understand the value of truth, we recognize that there is no difference between the needs of individuals and the need of whole communities. Their numbers vary but their desire and right not to be deceived remains the same. Thus when we commit ourselves to truth – and thereby to honesty – we help reduce the level of misunderstanding, doubt and fear throughout society. In a small but significant way, we create the conditions for a happy world.

The question of justice is also closely connected both with truth and the notion of universal responsibility. Justice entails a requirement to act when we become aware of injustice. Indeed, failure to do so may be wrong. Not wrong in the sense that it makes us somehow intrinsically bad. But if our hesitance to speak out comes from a sense of self-centredness, if our response is to ask 'What will happen to me if I speak out?' Or to worry, 'Maybe people won't like me.' This is not merely unethical in that we are ignoring the wider implications of our silence, but inappropriate and unhelpful when set in the context of all others' equal rights to have happiness and to avoid suffering. This remains true even – perhaps especially – when people say 'This is our business' or 'This is an internal affair.' Not only is speaking out under such circumstances a duty, more importantly, it can be a service to others.

It may of course be objected that such honesty is not always possible, that we need to be 'realistic'. Our circumstances may prevent us from always acting in accordance with our responsibilities. Our own families may be harmed if, for example, we speak out when we witness injustice. But whilst we do, of course, have to deal with the day to day reality of our lives, it is essential to keep this in perspective. We must evaluate our own needs in relation to the needs of others and consider how our actions and omissions are likely to affect them in the longer term. It is hard to criticize those who fear for their loved ones. But occasionally it will be necessary to take risks in order to benefit the wider community.

A sense of responsibility towards others also means that both as individuals and as a society of individuals, we have a duty of care to each member of our society. This is true irrespective of either their physical capacity or of their capacity for mental reflection. Just like ourselves, such people have a right to happiness and to avoid suffering. We must therefore avoid, at all cost, the urge to shut away those who are grievously afflicted as if they were a burden. The same goes for those who are diseased or marginalized. To do so would be to heap suffering on suffering. If we ourselves were in the same condition, we would look to others for help. We need therefore to ensure that the sick and afflicted person never feels helpless, rejected or unprotected. Indeed, the affection we show to such people is, in my opinion, the measure of our spiritual health, both at the level of the individual and at that of society.

All this talk of universal responsibility and what it entails may sound hopelessly idealistic on my part. Nevertheless, it is an idea I have been expressing publicly ever since my first trips to the West, in the 1970's. In those days, many people were sceptical of such notions. Similarly, it was not always easy to interest people in the concept of world peace. I am encouraged to note that today, however, an increasing number are beginning to respond favourably to these ideas. As a result of the many extraordinary events humanity has experienced during the course of the twentieth century, we have, I feel, become more mature. In the fifties and sixties, and in some places even more recently, many people felt ultimately that, conflicts should be resolved through war. Today, that thinking holds sway only in the minds of a small minority. Whereas in the early part of this century many people believed that progress and development within society should be pursued through strict regimentation, the collapse of fascism followed later by the disappearance of the so-called Iron Curtain, has shown this to be a hopeless enterprise. Moreover, for almost a century now there has been a consensus – amongst some Buddhists too – that science and spirituality are incompatible. Today, as the scientific understanding of the nature of reality deepens, this perception is changing. Because of this, people are beginning to show more interest in what I have called our inner world. By this I mean the dynamics and functions of consciousness, or spirit. In addition, there is the worldwide increase in environmental awareness. To me, these are all very encouraging developments. They are sure to have far reaching consequences. So too is the growing awareness that neither individuals nor even whole nations can solve all their problems by themselves, that we need one another. I am also encouraged by the fact that regardless of its implementation, there is at least clearer acknowledgement of the need to seek non-violent resolutions to conflict in a spirit of reconciliation. There is also, as we have noted, growing acceptance of the universality of human rights and indeed of the need to accept diversity in areas of common importance, such as in religious affairs. This I believe to reflect a recognition of the need for a wider perspective in response to the diversity of the human family itself. As a result, despite the amount of suffering that continues to be inflicted on individuals and peoples in the name of ideology, religion, progress, development, and economics, a new sense of hope is emerging for the downtrodden. Although it will undoubtedly be difficult to bring about genuine peace and harmony, clearly it can be done. The potential is there. And its foundation is a sense of responsibility on the part of each individual towards all others.

CHAPTER TWELVE

LEVELS OF COMMITMENT

Through developing an attitude of responsibility towards others, we can begin to create the kinder, more compassionate world we all dream of. Given that there are several areas of human endeavour where such an attitude is especially relevant, we need to ensure that it informs our activities not merely at the level of the individual, however. It is also essential at the level of society itself. Inter-religious harmony, international peace, our natural environment, politics and economics and the fields of education and the media each require that we consider others' interests alongside our own.

We will briefly examine each of these in turn. But

before doing so, I should perhaps explain my personal point of view with respect to the question of commitment to the principle of universal responsibility. First of all, I trust it is clear that I am not calling on everyone to renounce their present way of life and adopt a new rule or way of thinking. Rather, my intention is to suggest that the individual, keeping his or her daily life, can change, can become a better – more compassionate and happier – human being. And through being better, more compassionate individuals, we can make a significant contribution to society itself.

This means that, just because a person may be working for a salary even in some humble occupation does not mean their work is any less relevant to the well-being of society than that of, for example, a doctor, a teacher, a monk or a nun. So long as we carry out our work with good motivation, thinking: 'My work is for others'. It will be of benefit to the wider community. All human endeavour is potentially great and noble. It is only when concern for others' feelings and welfare are missing that our activities become spoiled. Through lack of basic human feeling, religion, politics, economics are rendered dirty. Instead of serving humanity, they become agents of its destruction. Therefore, in addition to developing a sense of universal responsibility, we need actually to be responsible people. Until we put our principles into practise, they remain just that. So, for example, politicians who are genuinely responsible must conduct themselves with honesty and integrity. A businessman or woman must consider the needs of others in every enterprise they undertake. A lawyer must use his or her expertise to fight for justice.

But in the same way that it is difficult to correlate degrees of religious belief with levels of spiritual attainment, so it is difficult to say that if our commitment to the principle of universal responsibility is this great, we should act in such-and-such a way. For this reason, I do not have any particular standard in mind. All that I hope is that, if what is written here makes sense to you the reader, you will incorporate the principle of non-harming into your daily life. And, out of a sense of responsibility towards others do what you can to help them. When you walk past a dripping tap, you will turn it off. If you see a light burning unnecessarily, you will do the same. If you are a religious practitioner and tomorrow you meet someone of another religious tradition, you will show them the same respect as you would hope them to show you. Or if you are a scientist and you see the possibility of the research you are engaged in disturbing others, out of a sense of responsibility, you will desist from it. According to your own resources, and recognizing the limitations of your circumstances, you will do what you can. Apart from this, I am not calling for any commitment as such. And if some days you implement these principles but on others you do not, well, that is normal. Likewise, if what I say does not seem helpful, then no matter. The important thing is that whatever we do for others, whatever sacrifices we make, it should be voluntary and arise from understanding the benefit of such actions.

Saying this, I do not mean to imply that, in terms of lifestyle, 'anything goes'. On a recent visit to New York, a friend told me that the number of billionaires in America had increased from seventeen just a few years ago to more than 350 today. So clearly the number of rich people in the world is growing. Yet at the same time, the poor remain poor and in some cases are becoming poorer. This I consider to be completely immoral. It is also potentially a source of problems. Whilst millions do not even have the basic necessities of life – adequate food, shelter, education and medical facilities – the inequity of wealth distribution is a scandal. If it were the case that everyone had sufficient for their needs and more, then perhaps a luxurious lifestyle would be tenable. If that was what the individual really wanted, it would be difficult to argue that they need refrain from exercising their right to live as they see fit. Yet things are not like that. In this one world of ours, there are areas where people throw food away while others – our fellow humans, innocent children among them – are reduced to scavenging among rubbish and starvation. Thus, although I cannot say that the life of luxury led by the rich is wrong of itself, assuming they are using their own money and have not acquired it dishonestly, I do say that it is unworthy, that it spoils us.

Moreover, it strikes me that the lifestyles of the rich are often absurdly and pointlessly complicated. One friend of mine, who stayed with an extremely wealthy family, told me that every time he went swimming, he was handed a bathing robe to wear. This would then be changed for a fresh one each time he used the pool, even if he did so several times in one day. Extraordinary! Ridiculous even. So complicated! It is not as if living like this adds anything to one's comfort. As human beings we have only one stomach. There is a limit to the amount we can eat. Similarly, we have only eight fingers and two thumbs. We cannot wear a hundred rings. Whatever extra we have is to no purpose in the moment when we are actually wearing a ring. The rest lie useless in their boxes. The appropriate use of wealth, as I explained to the members of one very prosperous Indian family who came to see me not long ago, is found in philanthropic giving. In this particular case, I suggested – since they asked – that spending on education is perhaps of most use. The future of the world is in our children's hands. Therefore, if we wish to bring about a more compassionate – and therefore fairer society – it is essential that we educate our children to be responsible, caring human beings. When a person is born rich, or acquires wealth by some other means, they have a tremendous opportunity to benefit others. What a waste it is when that opportunity is squandered on self-indulgence.

I feel strongly that luxurious living is inappropriate,

so much so that I must admit that whenever I stay in a comfortable hotel and see others eating and drinking expensively whilst there are people outside who do not even have anywhere to spend the night, I feel greatly disturbed. It reminds me that I am no different from either the rich or the poor. We are the same in wanting happiness and not to suffer. And we have an equal right to that happiness. But because of different circumstances, the rich have disproportionately more than the poor. As a result, I feel that if I were to see a workers' demonstration going by, I would certainly join in. And yet the person who is saying these things is one of those enjoying the comforts of the hotel. Indeed, I must go further. It is also true that I possess several valuable wrist watches. I sometimes feel that if I were to sell them I could perhaps build some huts for the poor, so far I have not. In the same way, I do feel that if I were to observe a strictly vegetarian diet not only would I be setting a better example, but I would also be helping to save innocent animals' lives. So I must admit a contradiction between my principles and my practice in certain areas. At the same time, I do not believe everyone can or should be like Mahatma Gandhi and live the life of a poor peasant. Such dedication is wonderful and greatly to be admired. But the watchword is: 'As much as possible', without going to extremes.

CHAPTER THIRTEEN

PEACE AND DISARMAMENT

Chairman Mao once said that political power comes from the barrel of a gun. Of course, it is true violence can achieve certain short-term objectives. But it cannot obtain long-lasting ends. If we look at history, we find that in time, humanity's love of peace, justice and truth always triumphs over cruelty and oppression. This is why I am such a fervent believer in non-violence. Violence begets violence. And violence means only one thing: suffering. Theoretically, of course, it is possible to conceive of a situation where the only way to prevent large scale conflict is through armed intervention at an early stage. The problem with this line of argument is that it is very difficult, if not impossible, to predict the outcome of violence. Nor can we be sure of its justness at the outset. This only becomes clear when we have the benefit of hindsight. The only certainty is that where there is violence suffering is inevitable.

Some people will say that whilst the Dalai Lama's devotion to non-violence is praiseworthy, it is not really practical. Actually, it is far more naive to suppose that the man-made problems which lead to violence can ever be solved through conflict. Observe, too that non-violence was the principle characteristic of the political revolutions which swept across so much of the world during the 1980's. One of the most hopeful aspects of the modern age is the emergence of an international peace movement. If we hear less about it today than we did at the end of the Cold War, it is perhaps because its ideals have been absorbed into mainstream consciousness.

I am convinced that the main reason so many people say the path of non-violence is impractical is because the task seems so daunting: we become discouraged. Nevertheless, whereas formerly it was enough to wish for peace in one's own land, or even just in one's neighbourhood, today we speak of world peace. This is only appropriate. The fact of human interdependence is so explicit now: the only peace it is meaningful to speak of is world peace.

But what do I mean when I speak of peace? Are there not grounds for supposing that war is a natural, if regrettable, human activity? Here we need to make a distinction between peace as a mere absence of war and peace as a state of tranquillity founded on the deep sense of security that arises from mutual understanding, tolerance of others' points of view and respect for their rights. Peace in this sense is not what we saw in Europe during the four and a half decades of Cold War, for example. That was only an approximation. The very premise on which it rested was fear and suspicion and the strange psychology of mutually assured destruction – aptly abbreviated to MAD. Indeed, the 'peace' which characterized the Cold War was so precarious, so fragile, that any serious misunderstanding on the part of either side could have had disastrous consequences. Looking back, especially with the knowledge we now have of the chaotic management of weapons systems in some quarters, I think it quite miraculous that we somehow escaped destruction!

Peace is not something which exists independently of us, any more than war does. It is true that certain individuals – political leaders, policymakers, army generals – have particularly heavy responsibilities in respect of peace. However, these people do not come from nowhere. They are not born and brought up in outer space. Like us, they were nourished by their mother's milk and shown affection. They are members of our own human family and have been nurtured within the society which we as individuals have helped create. Peace in the world thus depends on peace in the hearts of individuals. This in turn depends on all of us maintaining ethics by disciplining our response to negative thoughts and emotions, and developing basic spiritual qualities.

If real peace is something more profound than a fragile equilibrium based on mutual hostility, if it ultimately depends on the resolution of internal conflict, what are we to say about war? Although paradoxically the aim of most military campaigns is peace, in reality, war is like fire in the human community, one whose fuel is living people. It also strongly resembles fire in the way it spreads. If, for example, we look at the course of the recent conflict in former Yugoslavia, we see that what began as a relatively confined dispute grew quickly to engulf the whole region. Similarly, if we look at individual battles, we see that if commanders perceive areas of weakness, they respond by sending in reinforcements – which is exactly like throwing live people onto a bonfire. But because of habituation, we ignore this. We fail to acknowledge that the very nature of war is cold cruelty and suffering.

The unfortunate truth is that we are conditioned to regard warfare as something exciting and even glamorous: the soldiers in smart uniforms (so attractive to children), with their military bands playing alongside them. We see murder as dreadful, but there is no association of war with criminality. On the contrary, it is seen as an opportunity for people to prove their competence and courage. We speak of the heros it produces: almost as if the greater the number killed, the more heroic the individual. We talk about this or that weapon as marvellous piece of technology, forgetting that when it is used it will actually maim and murder living people. Your friend, my friend, our fathers, our mothers, our sisters and brothers, you and me.

What is even worse is the fact that, in modern warfare, the role of the people prosecuting it is diminishing further and further. At the same time, its impact on non-combatants grows ever greater. Those who suffer most in today's armed conflicts are the innocent – not only the families of those fighting but, in far greater numbers civilians who often do not even have a direct role. Even after the war is over, enormous suffering continues due to land-mines, poisoning from the use of chemical weapons, and the economic hardship war brings. For this reason, I see no reason to doubt the assertion that the ratio of civilian to military casualties is of the order of nine to one. This means that women, children and the elderly are in fact the prime victims of war.

Moreover, the ever-increasing sophistication of wea-ponry has outrun the imaginative capacity of the average lay person. The destructive capacity of modern warfare is so astonishing that, whatever arguments there may be in favour of war, they must be vastly inferior to those against. We could be forgiven for feeling nostalgia for the warfare of ancient times. At least then when people fought one another they did so face to face. There was no denying the suffering involved. And in those days, it was usual for rulers to lead their troops in battle. If he was killed, that was often the end of the matter. But as technology improved, so the generals began to stay further and further behind. Today they can be thousands of miles away in their bunkers underground conducting battles almost as if they were a computer game. In view of this, I personally would welcome a 'smart' bullet that could seek out and kill those who decide on wars in the first place. That would seem to me more fair – a weapon that eliminated the decision makers whilst leaving the innocent unharmed. Such a device seems especially appropriate in this nuclear age of ours where there can be no ultimate victor.

Because of the reality of this destructive capacity, we need to admit that, whether they are intended for offensive, or for defensive purposes, weapons exist solely to destroy human beings. They are the oxygen of conflict. But lest we suppose that peace is purely dependent upon disarmament, we must also acknowledge that weapons cannot act by themselves. Although designed to kill, so long as they remain in storage, they can do no physical harm. Someone has to touch a button to launch a missile strike, or pull a trigger to fire a bullet. No evil power can do this. Only humans can. Therefore, genuine world peace requires that we also begin to dismantle the military establishments that we have built. We cannot hope to enjoy peace in its fullest sense whilst it remains possible for a few individuals to exercise military power and impose their will on others. Nor, for that matter, can we hope to enjoy true peace as long as there are authoritarian regimes propped up by their armed forces which do not hesitate to carry out injustice at their bidding. This is because injustice undermines truth, and without truth there can be no lasting peace. Why not? Because when we have truth on our side, there is a straightforwardness, a confidence that comes with it. Conversely, where truth is lacking, the only way we can achieve our narrow aims is through force. When decisions come about this way, in defiance of truth, people do not feel quite right – either the victors or the vanquished. This negative feeling serves to undermine the peace which is imposed by force.

Clearly we cannot hope to achieve military disestablishment overnight, however. And whilst our ultimate goal, if we wish to see a society in which armed conflict becomes a thing of the past, must be the abolition of all military apparatus. Clearly it is too much to hope for the elimination of all weapons. There will always be groups of troublemakers and fanatics who will cause disturbance for others. Therefore, we must allow that so long as there are human beings, there will have to be ways of dealing with miscreants. At the same time, we need to establish clear objectives in respect of what is possible and begin to develop the political will to move towards them.

We each have a role to play in this. If, as individuals, we disarm ourselves internally – through disciplining our negative thoughts and emotions and cultivating positive qualities – we create the conditions for external disarmament. Indeed, genuine, lasting world peace will only be possible as a result of each of us making an effort internally. It is thus essential that we remain sensitive to others and, recognizing their equal rights to happiness, do nothing that could contribute to their suffering. To help us in this, it is useful to take time and reflect on how war is actually experienced by its victims. For my own part, I have only to think of my visit to Hiroshima some years ago to bring to life war's full horror. In the museum there, I saw a watch that had stopped at the exact moment the bomb exploded. I also saw a small packet of sewing needles, the contents of which had been fused together in the explosion's heat.

With respect to the practical measures required to bring about military disestablishment, we need to recognize that it can only occur within the context of a broad commitment to disarmament. It is not enough to think merely in terms of eliminating our weapons of mass destruction. We must create the conditions favourable to our objective. The most obvious way of doing this is through building on existing initiatives. Here I am thinking of the efforts over many years to exercise control over the proliferation of certain classes of weapon – and in some cases to eliminate them. During the 1970's and 1980's, we saw the Strategic Arms Limitation Treaties between the Eastern and Western blocs. We have had in place for many years a nuclear non-proliferation treaty to which many countries are already commited. And despite the spread of nuclear weapons, the idea of a universal ban is still alive. Encouraging progress has also been made towards the banning of land-mines. A majority of the world's governments have signed protocols renouncing their use. So whilst it remains true that none of these initiatives have fully succeeded in their aims, their very existence indicates recognition of the undesirability of these methods of destruction. They testify to humanity's basic wish to live in peace, and they provide a useful starting point.

Another way in which we can move further towards our objective of global military disestablishment is through gradually dismantling our arms industry. To many, this suggestion will seem a preposterous and unfeasible idea. They will object that this would be madness unless everybody agrees to do so simultaneously. And that, they will say, can never happen. Besides, they will add, there is the economic argument to consider. Yet if we look at the matter from the point of view of those who suffer the consequences of armed violence, it becomes very hard to deny our responsibility to overcome these objections by some means or another. Indeed, whenever I think of the arms industry and the suffering it enables, I am again reminded of my visit to the Nazi death camp at Auschwitz. As I stood looking at the ovens in which thousands of human beings just like myself were burned – many of them still alive – humans who cannot bear the heat of a single match – what struck me hardest was the realization that these devices had been built with the care and attention of talented workmen. I could almost see the engineers (all intelligent people) at their drawing boards, carefully planning the shape of the combustion chambers and calculating the size of chimneys, their height and breadth. I thought of the craftsmen who brought the design to fruition. No doubt they took pride in their work, as good craftsmen do. Then it occured to me that this is precisely what modern day weapons designers and manufacturers are about. They too are devising the means to destroy thousands if not millions of their fellow human beings. Isn't this a disturbing thought?

With this in mind, all individuals who undertake such work would do well to consider whether they can really justify their involvement. No doubt they would suffer if they gave it up unilaterally. No doubt, too, the economies of the arms manufacturing nations would suffer if these facilities were closed down. But would not this be a price worth paying? Besides, it seems that there are many examples in the world of companies which have successfully converted from weapons to some other form of manufacture. Also, we have the example of the world's one demilitarized state which we can consider in relation to its neighbours. If the example of Costa Rica which disarmed as long ago as 1949, is anything to go by, the benefits in terms of standard of living, of health and education are tremendous.

As to the argument that it would perhaps be more realistic simply to restrict arms exports to those countries which are reliable and safe, I suggest that this reflects a very short-sighted outlook. It has been demonstrated time and time again that this does not work. We are all familiar with the recent history of the Persian Gulf. During the 1970's, the Western allies armed the Shah of Iran as a counterforce to the perceived threat from the former Soviet Union. When the political climate changed, Iran itself was considered a threat to Western interests. The allies began to arm Iraq against Iran. But then, when times changed yet again, these weapons were used against the West's other allies in the Gulf (Kuwait). As a result the manufacturing countries found themselves going to war with their own client. In other words, there is no such thing as a 'safe' client for arms.

I cannot deny that my hope for global disarmament and military disestablishment are idealistic. At the same time, there are clear grounds for optimism. One is the ironic fact that, as far as nuclear and other weapons of mass destruction are concerned, it is extremely hard to conceive of a situation in which they could be useful. Nobody wants to risk the inevitable outcome of all out nuclear war. Second, these weapons are an obvious waste of money. In the first place, they are expensive to produce. Then, because to all intents and purposes it is impossible to imagine using them, there is nothing to do but stockpile them, which also costs a great deal of money. In effect, therefore, they are utterly useless and nothing but a drain on resources.

Where there are human beings, there will always be conflict, this is true. Disagreements are bound to surface from time to time. But given today's reality, we have to find some way other than violence to resolve them. This means dialogue in the spirit of reconciliation and compromise. This is not just wishful thinking on my part. Another reason for optimism is the steady intertwining of national economies. This is creating a climate in which notions of purely national interest and advantage are becoming less and less meaningful. As a result, the idea of using war as means to resolve conflict is starting to look decidedly old-fashioned. The global trend towards international political grouping, of which the European Union is the most obvious example, means that it is poss- ible to envisage a time when maintaining purely national standing armies could one day come to seem both uneco- nomic and unnecessary. Instead of thinking only in terms of protecting individual borders, it will become logical to think in terms of regional security. In fact it is clear that this is already beginning to happen. There are, albeit as yet tentative, plans to integrate European defences more closely; a Franco–German army brigade has been in exist- ence for more than ten years now. It thus seems possible, at least so far as the European Union is concerned, that what began purely as a trading alliance could eventually come to assume responsibility for regional security. And if this is possible within Europe, there is reason to hope that other international trading groups – of which there are many – could evolve to do the same. Why not?

The emergence of such regional security groupings would, I feel, contribute enormously to the transition from our current preoccupation with nation states to the gradual acceptance of less narrowly defined communities. They could eventually pave the way to a world in which there would be no standing armies at all. Such a scenario would of course have to evolve in stages. First national armed forces would give way to regional security groupings. These could then gradually be disbanded leaving only to a globally administered police force. The main purpose of this force would be to safeguard justice, communal security and human rights worldwide. Its specific duties would be various, however. Protecting against the appropriation of power by violent means would be one of them. As to its operation, I imagine that it could be called in by communities which came under threat – from neighbours or from a minority of its own members, such as a violently extreme political faction – or it could be deployed by the international community itself when violence seemed the likely outcome of conflict, to resolve religious or ideological disputes.

Although it is true that we are a long way from this ideal situation, again it is not as fanciful as it may at first seem. This generation may not live to see it. But we are already accustomed to seeing United Nations troops deployed as peacekeepers. We are also beginning to see the emergence of a consensus that it may be justifiable to use them in a more interventionist way under certain circumstances.

As a means for furthering these developments we might consider the establishment of what I call Zones of Peace. Here I imagine either a part or parts of one or more country being demilitarized to create oases of stability, preferably in areas of strategic significance. These would the serve as beacons of hope for the rest of the world. Admittedly this idea is quite ambitious, but it is not without precedent. We already have one such internationally recognised demilitarized zone in Antarctica. Nor am I the only individual ever to suggest there could be more. The former Russian President, Mikhail Gorbachev proposed just such status for the Sino–Russian border area. I myself have advanced the idea in respect of Tibet.

Of course, it is not hard to think of areas in the world other than the Tibet where neighbouring communities would benefit enormously from the establishment of a demilitarized zone. Just as India and China would save a considerable proportion of their respective annual income, there are many others on each continent from which a tremendous, wasteful, burden would be lifted if there were no need to maintain large numbers of troops on their borders. I have often thought, for example, that Germany is a most appropriate location for a Zone of Peace, lying as it does in the heart of Europe and taking into account the experience of the twentieth century's two world wars.

In all of this, I believe the United Nations has a critical role to play. Not that it is the only body devoted to global issues. There is also much to admire about the ethic behind others such as the International Court at the Hague, the International Monetary Fund, the World Bank and those dedicated to upholding the Geneva Convention. But at present, and for the conceivable future, the UN is the only global institution capable of influencing and formulating policy on behalf of the international community. Of course, many people criticize it on the grounds that it is ineffective, and it is true that time and again we have seen its resolutions ignored, abandoned and forgotten. Nevertheless, in spite of these shortcomings, I for one continue to have the highest regard not only for the principles on which it was founded but also for the great deal it has achieved since its inception in 1945. We need only ask ourselves whether or not it has helped save lives through diffusing potentially disastrous situations to see that it is more than the toothless bureaucracy some people say it is. We should also consider the great work of its subsidiary organisations, such as UNICEF, UNESCO, United Nations High Commission for Refugees and also the World Health Organization. This remains true even if some of their programmes and policies have been flawed and misguided.

I see the UN as being the proper vehicle for carrying out the wishes of humanity as a whole. As yet it is not able to do this very effectively, but we are only just beginning to see the emergence of a global consciousness – which has been made possible by the communications revolution. In spite of tremendous difficulties, we have seen it in action in numerous parts of the world. Even though there are only one or two nations spearheading these initiatives at the moment, the fact that they are seeking the legitimacy conferred by a United Nations mandate suggests a felt need for justification through collective approbation. This, in turn, I believe to be indicative of a growing sense of a single, mutually dependent, human community.

Although it provides a forum for individual governments, one of the particular weaknesses of the United Nations as it is presently constituted is that individual citizens cannot be heard there. It has no mechanism whereby those wishing to speak out against their own governments can be heard. To make matters worse, the way in which the veto system works means that it is open to manipulation by the more powerful nations. These are profound shortcomings. The injustice of the present veto system could quite easily be overcome, however. If, for example, every state had the power to veto but a two-thirds majority could overrule it, that would be significantly more democratic.

As to the problem of individuals not having a voice, here we might have to consider something more radical. Just as in each country, democracy is ensured by the three pillars of independent judiciary, and executive and legislative branches, so we need to have a genuinely independent body at international level. But perhaps the United Nations is not entirely suited to this role. I have noticed at international gatherings, such as the Earth Summit in Brazil, that individuals who come to represent their governments, inevitably put the interests of their nation first. This despite the fact that the question at issue transcends national boundaries. Conversely, where people come as individuals to international gatherings – such as the Physicians for Social Responsibility, or indeed the initiative on the arms trade by the Nobel Peace Laureates, of which I am a member – there is much greater concern for humanity itself. The spirit of such gatherings is much more genuinely international and open. This leads me to think that it could be worthwhile to establish a body whose principle task would be to monitor human affairs from the perspective of ethics. What I have in mind here is an organization that might be called the World Council of the People (although no doubt a better name could be found). This would consist of an elected group of individuals drawn, as I imagine it, from a wide variety of backgrounds. There would be artists, bankers, environmentalists, lawyers, poets, academics, religious thinkers, writers as well as ordinary men and women with a common reputation for integrity and dedication to fundamental ethical and human values. Because this body would not actually be invested with political power, its pronouncements would not be legally binding. But by virtue of its independence, having no link with any one nation or group of nations, and no ideology, these deliberations would be seen to represent the conscience of the world. They would thus carry moral authority.

Of course, there will be many who criticize this proposal, along with what I have said about military disestablishment, disarmament and reform of the United Nations on the grounds that it is unrealistic, or perhaps just too simplistic. Or they will say that it is not workable in 'the real world'. Whilst people are often content to just criticize and blame others for what goes wrong, surely we should at least attempt to put forward constructive ideas? One thing is for certain. Given human beings' love of peace, truth, justice, and freedom, creating a better, more compassionate world is a genuine possibility. The potential is there. If, with the help of education and the proper use of the media we can combine some of the initiatives suggested here with the implementation of ethical principles, we will have within our reach a climate in which disarmament and military disestablishment become totally uncontroversial. On this basis we will have created the conditions for lasting world peace.

CHAPTER FOURTEEN

FURTHER
RESPONSIBILITIES

EDUCATION AND THE MEDIA

Whether visiting one of our schools for Tibetan refugees in India or speaking to student audiences abroad, I am always very happy to meet young people. They have a natural enthusiasm for justice and peace, and they tend to be much more open and flexible of mind than adults. No matter how well disposed towards change we are, we adults undoubtedly find it more difficult. Meeting the young also reminds me that children constitute humanity's most precious resource. Given that their moral outlook is largely shaped by their upbringing, it is essential we educate them responsibly.

The human mind (*lo*) is both the source and, properly directed, the solution to all our problems. Those who attain great learning but lack a good heart are in danger of falling prey to the anxieties and restlessness which result from desires incapable of fulfilment. This is because what I call material knowledge can easily be a source of negative thoughts and feelings. Conversely, a genuine understanding of spiritual values brings peace. If we bring up our children to have knowledge without the compassion, their attitude towards others is likely to be a mixture of envy of those in positions above them, aggressive competitiveness towards their peers and scorn for those less fortunate. This leads to a propensity towards greed, presumption, excess and, very quickly, to loss of happiness. Knowledge is important, but much more important is the use towards which it is put. This depends on the heart and mind of the one who uses it.

Education is therefore much more than a matter of imparting the knowledge and skills by which narrow goals are achieved. It is also about opening the child's eyes to the needs and rights of others. We must show them that their actions have a universal dimension. And we must somehow find a way to build on their natural feelings of empathy in such a way that they come to have a sense of responsibility towards others. For it is this which stirs us into action. Indeed, if we had to choose between learning and virtue, the latter is definitely more valuable. The good heart which is the fruit of virtue is by itself a great benefit to humanity. Mere knowledge is not.

How, though, are we to teach morality to our children? I have a sense that, in general, modern education systems neglect discussion of ethical matters. This is probably not intentional as much as it is a by-product of historical reality. Most modern secular education systems were developed at a time when religious institutions were still highly influential throughout society. Because ethical and human values were and still are generally held to fall within the purview of religion, it was assumed that this aspect of a child's education would be looked after through his or her religious upbringing. This worked well enough until the influence of religion began to decline. Although the need is still there, it is not being met. Therefore, we must find another way of showing children that basic human values are important. And we must also help children to develop them.

Ultimately, of course, the importance of concern for others is learned not from words but from actions: the example we set. This is why the family environment is such a vital component in a child's upbringing. Where a caring and compassionate atmosphere is absent from the home, where children are neglected by their parents, it is easy to recognise them. They feel helpless and insecure and their minds are often agitated. Conversely, if children receive constant affection and protection, they tend to be much happier and more confident in their abilities. Their physical health tends to be better too. We find that they are concerned not just for themselves but for others as well. The home environment is also important where children learn negative behaviour from their parents. If, for example, the father is always getting into fights with his associates, or if father and mother are always arguing, although at first the child may find this objectionable, eventually they come to understand it as quite normal. This learning is then taken out of the home and into the world.

It also goes without saying that, what children learn about ethical conduct has to be practised first. In this, teachers have a special responsibility. By their own behaviour, teachers can make children remember them for their whole lives. If this is principled, disciplined, and compassionate, their values will be readily impressed on the child's mind. This is because the lessons taught by a teacher with a positive motivation (*kun-long*) go deepest into their students' minds. I know this from my own experience. As a boy, I was very lazy. But if I was aware of my tutors' affection and concern, their lessons would generally sink in much more successfully than if one of them was harsh or unfeeling that day.

As far as the specifics of education are concerned, that is for the experts. I will therefore confine myself to a few suggestions. The first is that: in order to awaken young peoples' consciousness to the importance of basic human values, best we do not present society's problems as an ethical matter, still less as a religious matter. Better by far is to present these problems in terms of the question of survival. This way, they will come to see that the future lies in their hands. Secondly, I do believe that dialogue can and should be taught in class. Presenting students with a controversial issue and having them debate it is a wonderful way to introduce them to the concept of conflict resolution. Indeed, one might hope that if schools were to make this a priority, it might have a beneficial effect on family life itself. On seeing his or her parents wrangling, a child who had understood the value of dialogue would instinctively say 'Oh no. That's not the way. You have to talk, to discuss things properly.'

Finally, it is essential that we eliminate from our schools' curricula any tendency towards presenting others in a negative light. There are undoubtedly some parts of the world where the teaching of history, for example, fosters bigotry and racism towards other communities. Of course this is wrong. It contributes nothing to the happiness of humanity. Now more than ever we need to show our children that distinctions between 'my country' and 'your country', 'my religion' and 'your religion', are secondary considerations. Rather, we must insist on the observation that my right to happiness carries no more weight than another's right. This is not to say that

ANCIENT WISDOM, MODERN WORLD

I believe we should educate children to abandon or ignore the culture and historical traditions into which they are born. On the contrary, it is very important that they be grounded in these. It is good for children to learn to love their country, their religion, their culture and so on. The danger comes when this develops into narrow-minded nationalism, ethnocentricity and religious bigotry. In this context, the example of Mahatma Gandhi is a good one. Even though he had a very high level of Western education, he never forgot or became estranged from the rich heritage of his Indian culture.

If education constitutes one of our most powerful weapons in our quest to bring about a better, more peaceful world, the mass media is another. As every political figure knows, they are no longer the only ones with authority over society. Film and television, newspapers, books and radio together have an influence over individuals that was unimagined a hundred years ago. This power confers great responsibility on all who work in the media. It also confers great responsibility on each of us who, as individuals, listen and read and watch. We too have a role to play. It is not the case that we have no power over what we take from the media. The control switch is in our own hands after all.

This does not mean that I advocate bland reporting or entertainment without excitement. On the contrary, so far as investigative journalism is concerned, I respect and appreciate the media's interference. Unfortunately, but inevitably, not all public servants are honest in discharging their duties. It is appropriate, therefore, to have journalists. Their noses are as long as an elephants trunk, snooping around and exposing wrong-doing where they find it. We need to know, therefore, when this or that renowned individual hides a very different aspect behind a pleasant exterior. There should be no discrepancy between external appearances and the individual's inner life. It is the same person after all. So where they exist, such discrepancies suggest them to be untrustworthy. At the same time, it is vital that the investigator does not act on the impulse of improper motives. Without impartiality and due regard for the other's rights, the investigation itself becomes tainted.

With regard to the question of the media's emphasis on sex and violence, there are many factors to consider. In the first instance, it is clear that much of the viewing public enjoys the sensations provoked by this sort of material. Secondly, I very much doubt that those producing material containing alot of explicit sex and violence intend harm by it. Their motives are surely just commercial. As to whether this is positive or negative in itself is to my mind less important than the question of whether it can have an ethically wholesome effect. If the result of seeing a film in which there is a lot of violence is that the viewer's compassion is aroused, then perhaps that depiction of violence would be justified. But if the accumulation of violent images leads to indifference, then

I think it is not. Indeed, such a hardening of heart is potentially dangerous. It leads all too easily to indifference.

When the media focuses too closely on the negative aspects of human nature, there is a danger that we become persuaded that violence and aggression are its principle characteristics. This is mistaken. The fact that violence is newsworthy suggests the very opposite. Good news is not remarked on precisely because there is so much of it. Consider that, at any given moment, there must be hundreds of millions of acts of kindness taking place around the world. Although there will undoubtedly be many acts of violence in progress at the same time, their number is certainly less. If, therefore, the media is to be ethically responsible, it needs to reflect this simple fact.

Clearly it is necessary to regulate the media. The fact that we prevent our children from watching certain things indicates that we do discriminate between what is and is not appropriate according to different circumstances. But whether legislation if the right way to go about this is hard to judge. As in all matters of ethics, discipline is only really effective when it comes from within. Perhaps the best way to ensure that the output of various media is healthy lies in the way we educate our children. If we bring them up to be aware of their responsibilities, they will be more disciplined if they become involved in the media.

Although it is perhaps too much to hope that the media will actually promote the ideals and principles of compassion, we should at least be able to expect that those involved will take care if there is the potential for negative impact. There should be no room for incitement of negative acts such as racist violence. But beyond this, I don't know. Perhaps we might be able to find a way to connect more directly those who create stories for news and entertainment and the viewer, the reader and the listener.

THE NATURAL WORLD

If there is one area to which both education and the media have a special responsibility, it is, I believe, our natural environment. This responsibility has less to do with questions of right or wrong than it does with survival. Still less should it reflect any idea that the natural world is anything sacred or holy. The natural world is our home, it is where we live. It is therefore in our interest to look after it. This is only common sense. The size of our population and the power of science and technology have become such that they have a direct impact on nature. To put it another way, until now, Mother Earth has been able to tolerate our sloppy house habits. The stage has been reached at which she can no longer accept our behaviour in silence. The problems caused by environmental degradation can be seen as her response to our irresponsible behaviour. It is as if she is warning us that there are limits even to her tolerance.

Nowhere are the consequences of our failure to exercise discipline in the way we relate to our environment more apparent than in the case of present-day Tibet. It is no exaggeration to say that the Tibet I grew up in was a wildlife paradise. Every traveller who visited Tibet before the middle of the twentieth century remarked on the tremendous number of wild animals. Part of the reason for this, I believe, was that they were rarely hunted – except in the remotest areas where crops could not be grown. Indeed, it was customary for government officials to issue an annual proclamation protecting wildlife: 'Nobody,' it read, 'however humble or noble, shall harm or do violence to the creatures of the waters or the wild.' The only exceptions were rats and wolves.

As a young man, I recall seeing great numbers of different species whenever I travelled outside Lhasa. My chief memory of the three month journey across Tibet from my birthplace at Takster in the East to Lhasa where I was formally proclaimed Dalai Lama is of the wildlife we encountered along the way. Immense herds of *kiang* (wild asses) and *drong* (wild yak) freely roamed the great plains. Occasionally we would catch sight of shimmering herds of *gowa*, the shy Tibetan gazelle, of *wa*, the white-lipped deer or of *tso* our majestic antelope. I remember too my fascination for the little *chibi*, or pika, which would congregate on grassy areas. They were so friendly. I loved to watch the birds too: the dignified *gho* (the bearded eagle) soaring high above monasteries perched in the mountains; the flocks of geese (*nangbar*); and occasionally to hear the call of the *wookpa* (the long eared owl) at night.

Even in Lhasa, one did not feel in any way cut off from the natural world. In my rooms at the top of the Potala, the winter palace of the Dalai Lamas, I spent countless hours as a child studying the behaviour of the red-beaked *khyungkar* which nested in the crevices of its walls. And behind the Norbulingka, the summer palace, I often saw pairs of *trung trung* (Japanese black-necked cranes), birds which are for me the epitome of elegance and grace, that lived in the marshlands there. And all this is not to mention the crowning glory of Tibetan fauna: the bears and mountain foxes, the *chanku* (wolves) and *sazik* (the beautiful snow leopard), the gentle-faced giant panda, which is native to the border area between Tibet and China, and the *sik* (lynx) which struck terror into the hearts of the nomad farmer.

Sadly, this profusion of wildlife is no longer to be found. Partly due to hunting, but primarily due to loss of habitat. What remains half a century after Tibet's occupation is only a fraction of what there was. Without exception, every Tibetan I have spoken with who has been back to visit Tibet after an absence of forty or fifty years has reported on the striking absence of wildlife. Before wild animals would often come close to the house, today they are hardly anywhere to be seen. Equally troubling is the devastation of Tibet's forests. In the past, the hills were all thickly wooded. Those who have been back report that today they are clean-shaven like a monk's head. The government in Beijing has admitted that the tragic flooding of Western China, and further afield, is in part due to this. Yet I hear continuous reports of round-the-clock convoys of lorries carrying logs east out of Tibet. This is especially tragic given the country's mountainous terrain and harsh climate. It means that replanting requires sustained care and attention. Unfortunately there is little evidence of this.

None of this is to say that, historically, we Tibetans were deliberately 'conservationist'. We were not. The idea of something called pollution simply never occurred to us. There is no denying we were rather spoiled in this respect. A small population inhabited a very large area with clean dry air and an abundance of pure mountain water. Like an only child, no matter what we did, Mother Earth tolerated our behaviour. The result was we had no proper understanding of cleanliness and hygiene. People would spit or blow their nose in the street without giving it a second thought. Indeed, saying this, I recall one elderly Khampa, a former bodyguard who used to come each day to circumambulate my residence in Dharamsala (a popular devotion). Unfortunately, he suffered greatly from bronchitis. This was exacerbated by the incense he carried. At each corner, therefore, he would pause to cough and expectorate so ferociously that I sometimes wondered whether he had come to pray or just to spit!

This innocent attitude towards cleanliness meant that when we Tibetans came into exile, we were astonished to discover the existence of streams whose water is not drinkable.

Over the years since then, I have taken a closer interest in environmental issues. The Tibetan government in exile has paid particular attention to introducing our children to their responsibilities as residents of this fragile planet. And I never hesitate to speak out on the subject whenever I am given the opportunity. In particular, I always stress the need to consider how our actions affect the environment, and how they are likely to affect others. I admit that this is very often difficult to judge. We cannot say for sure what the ultimate effects of deforestation might be on the soil and the local rainfall, let alone what the implications are for the planet's weather systems. The only clear thing is that we humans are the only species with the power to destroy the earth as we know it. The birds have no such power, nor do the insects, nor does any mammal. Yet if we have the capacity to destroy the earth, so too do we have the capacity to protect it.

What is essential is that we find ways of achieving legitimate ends without harming the environment. We need to find methods of manufacture that do not destroy nature. We need to find ways of cutting down on our use of wood and other limited natural resources. I am no expert in this field and I cannot suggest how this might be done. I know only that it is possible, given the necessary determination. For example, while visiting Stockholm some years ago, I recall hearing that fish were returning to the river that runs through the city for the first time in many years. There had been none due to industrial pollution. Yet this improvement was by no means the result of all the local factories closing down. Likewise, on a visit to Germany I was shown an industrial development designed to produce no pollution. Clearly solutions do exist to limit damage to the natural world without bringing industry to a halt.

This does not mean that I believe we can rely on technology to overcome all our problems. Nor do I believe we can afford to continue destructive practices in anticipation of technical fixes being developed. Besides, the environment does not need fixing. It is our behaviour in relation to it that needs to change. Secondly, I question whether, in the case of such a massive looming disaster as that caused by the greenhouse effect, a 'fix' could ever exist, even in theory. And if it could, we have to ask whether it would be feasible to apply it on the scale that would be required. What of the expense and what of the cost in terms of our natural resources? I suspect that these would be prohibitively high. There is also the fact that in many other fields – such as in the humanitarian relief of hunger – there are already insufficient funds to cover the work that could be undertaken. Therefore, even if one were to argue that the necessary funds could be raised, morally speaking this would be almost impossible to justify given such deficiencies. It would not be right to deploy huge sums simply to enable the industrialized nations to continue their harmful practices whilst people in other places cannot even feed themselves.

All this points to the need to recognize the universal dimension of our actions and to exercise restraint based on this. The necessity of this is forcefully demonstrated when we come to consider the propagation of our species. Although it is the point of view of all the major religions that the more humans the better, and although it may be true that some of the latest studies suggest a population implosion a century from now, I still believe we cannot ignore this issue. Family planning is important. Human life is a precious resource. Therefore, married couples should have children unless there are compelling reasons not to. I think the idea of not having children just because we want to enjoy a full life without responsibility is just nonsense. But couples do have a duty to consider the impact our numbers have on the natural environment. This is especially true given the impact of modern technology.

Fortunately, more and more people are coming to recognize the importance of ethical discipline as a means to ensuring a healthy place to live. For this reason I am optimistic that disaster can be averted. Until comparatively recently, few people gave much thought to the effects of human activity on our planet. Yet today there are even political parties whose main concern it is. Moreover, the fact that the air we breathe, the water we drink, the forests and oceans which sustain millions of different life forms, and the climatic patterns which govern our weather systems all transcend national boundaries is a source of hope, I feel. It means that no country, no matter how powerful it may be, can afford not to take action in respect of this issue.

As far as the individual is concerned, the problems resulting from our neglect of our natural environment are a powerful reminder that each of us has a contribution to make. Whilst one person's actions may not have a significant impact, the combined effect of millions of individuals' actions certainly does. This means that it is time for all those living in the industrially developed nations to give serious thought to changing their lifestyle. Again this is not so much a question of ethics. I have suggested that luxurious living is both inappropriate and unworthy. But the fact that the population of the rest of the world has an equal right to improve their standard of living is in some ways more important. If this is to be fulfilled without causing irredeemable violence to the natural world – with all the negative consequences for happiness that this would entail – the richer countries must set an example. And they must recognize that their pursuit of ever increasing standards of living is unsustainable. The cost to the planet, and thus the cost to others is simply too great.

POLITICS AND ECONOMICS

During the last fifty years, we have witnessed an astounding increase in the financial wealth of the world. Yet although this has resulted in a standard of living higher than could ever have been imagined, it has been confined to a minority. There remains severe privation amongst perhaps half the world's population. Food, shelter, and medicine are in short supply amongst too many of our brothers and sisters. Our basic sense of justice and fairness alone suggests that we should not be content with the way things are progressing. If it seemed likely that, carrying on as we are, we could eradicate poverty after, say another fifty, or even after another hundred years, perhaps we would be justified in doing so. But this seems highly unlikely.

Of course I don't know much about economics. But I find it difficult not to suspect that, by means of international debt and the exploitation of natural resources at relatively low cost, the wealth of the rich is maintained through neglect of the poor. Saying this, I do not mean to suggest that the poorer countries have no share of responsibility for their problems. It is clear for example that many political leaders in these places are far more concerned for themselves than for their people. This narrow-mindedness is made worse still when it is translated into squandering slender resources on military equipment.

We cannot put all social and economic ills down to politicians and public officials, however. I do not deny that, even in the world's most established democracies it is quite usual to hear politicians boasting about what they are going to do when elected and making unrealistic promises to do this or that. But these people do not drop out of the sky. If it is true that a given country's politicians are corrupt, we will tend to find that society is itself lacking in morality, that the individuals who make up the population do not practise ethics in their own lives. In such cases, it is unjust of the electorate to criticize their politicians. On the other hand, if people possess healthy moral values, and if they practise ethical discipline in their own lives out of concern for others, the public officials produced by that society will quite naturally respect those same values. Each of us therefore has a role to play in creating a society based on empathy in which respect and care for others are given top priority.

As far as the application of economic policy is concerned, the same considerations apply here, as to every human activity. A sense of universal reponsibility is crucial. I must admit, however, that I find it a bit difficult to make practical suggestions concerning the application of spiritual values in the field of commerce. This is because competition has such as important role to play. For this reason, the relationship between empathy and profit is necessarily a fragile one. Still, I do not see why it should not be possible to have competition which is constructive. The key factor is the motivation of those engaged in it. If there is meanness or if the intention is to exploit others, then clearly the outcome will not be positive. But if competition is conducted within a spirit of generosity and good intention, the outcome, though it must entail a degree of suffering for those who lose, will not be too harmful at least.

Again it may be objected that the reality of commerce is such that we cannot realistically expect businesses to put people before profits. But we must remember that those who run the world's industries and businesses are human beings too. Even the most committed would surely admit that it is not right to seek profits regardless of consequences. If it were, dealing in drugs would not be wrong. So again, what is required is that each of us develop our compassionate nature. The more we do so, the more commercial enterprise will come to reflect basic human values. Conversely, if we ourselves neglect those values, it is inevitable that commerce will neglect them too. This is not just idealism. History shows that most of the positive or beneficial developments in human society have occurred as result of care and compassion. Consider, for example, the abolition of the slave trade. If we look at the evolution of human society, we see the necessity of having vision in order to bring about positive change. Ideals are the engine of progress. To ignore this and say merely that we need to be 'realistic' in politics is thus mistaken.

Our problems of economic disparity pose a very serious challenge to the whole human family. Nevertheless, as we enter the new millennium, I believe there are a good number of reasons for optimism. First of all, whilst it seems that during the early and middle years of the twentieth century, there was a general perception that political and economic power were of more consequence than truth in many parts of the world. Today we are witnessing a change. Even the wealthiest and most powerful nations understand that there is no point in neglecting basic human values. The notion that there is a room for ethics in international relations is also gaining ground. Irrespective of whether it is translated into meaningful action, at least words like 'reconciliation', 'non-violence' and 'compassion' are becoming stock phrases amongst politicians. This is a good beginning. It is my own experience that when I travel abroad I am quite often asked to speak about peace and compassion to quite large audiences – often in excess of a thousand. I doubt very much whether these topics would have attracted such numbers forty or fifty years ago. Developments such as these indicate that collectively we humans are giving more weight to fundamental values such as justice and truth.

I also take comfort from the fact that as the world economy evolves, the more explicitly interdependent it becomes. As a result, every nation is to a greater or lesser extent dependent on every other nation. The modern economy, like the environment, knows no boundaries. Even those countries openly hostile to one another must cooperate in their use of the world's resources. Often, for example, they will be dependent on the same rivers. And the more interdependent our economic relationships, the more interdependent must our political relationships become. Thus we have witnessed the growth of the European Union from a small caucus of trading partners into something approaching a confederation of states with a membership now well into double figures. We see similar, though presently less well-developed group-ings throughout the world: the Association of South East Asian Nations, the Organization for African Unity, the Organization of Petroleum Exporting Countries to name but three. Each of these testify to the human impulse to join together for the common good and reflect the continuing evolution of human society. What began with relatively small tribal units has progressed through the foundation of city states to nationhood and now to alliances comprising hundreds of millions of people, which increasingly transcend geographical, cultural and ethnic divisions. This is a trend which I believe will and must continue.

We cannot deny, however, that parallel to the proli-feration of these political and economic alliances, there is also a clear urge towards greater consolidation along the lines of ethnicity, language, religion and culture –

often in the context of violence following the loosening of the of the bonds of nation statehood. What are we to make of this seeming paradox – the trend towards transnational cooperative groupings on the one hand and the impulse towards localization on the other? In fact, there is not necessarily a contradiction between the two. We can still imagine regional communities united in trade, social policy and security arrangements that consist of a multiplicity of autonomous ethnic, cultural, religious and other groupings. There could be a legal system protecting basic human rights common to the larger community which leaves the constituent communities free to pursue their desired way of life. At the same time, it is important that if unions are established, they come about voluntarily and on the basis of recognition that the interests of those concerned are better served through collaboration. They must not be imposed. Indeed, the challenge of the new millennium is to find ways to achieve inter-national cooperation, or better, *intercommunity* wherein all human diversity is acknowledged and the rights of all are respected.

CHAPTER FIFTEEN

THE ROLE OF RELIGION IN MODERN SOCIETY

It is a sad fact of human history that religion has been a major source of conflict. Even today, individuals are killed, their communities destroyed and societies destabilized as a result of religious bigotry and hatred. It is no wonder that many question the place of religion in human affairs. Yet if we think carefully, we find that conflict in the name of religion arises from two principle sources. There is that which arises simply as a result of religious diversity – the doctrinal, cultural and practical differences between one religion and another. Then there is the conflict that arises in the context of political, economic and other factors, mainly at the institutional level. Inter-religious harmony is the key to overcoming conflict of the first sort. In the case of the second, some other solution must be found. Secularization and in particular the separation of the religious hierarchy from the offices of the state, may go some way to reducing such institutional problems. Our concern in this chapter is with inter-religious harmony, however.

This is an important aspect of what I have called universal responsibility. But before examining the matter in detail, it is perhaps worth considering the question of whether religion is really relevant in the modern world. Many people argue that it is not. Now I have observed that religious practice is not a precondition either of ethical conduct or of happiness itself. I have also suggested that, whether a person practises religion or not, the spiritual qualities of love and compassion, patience, tolerance, forgiveness, humility and so on are indispensable. At the same time, I should make clear that I believe that these are most easily and effectively developed within the context of religious practice. I also believe that if an individual sincerely practises religion, that individual will benefit enormously. People who have developed firm faith, grounded in understanding and rooted in daily practice, are, in general, much better at coping with adversity than those who have not. I am convinced, therefore, that religion has enormous potential to benefit humanity. Properly employed, it is an extremely effective instrument for establishing human happiness. In particular, it can play a leading role in encouraging people to develop a sense of responsibility towards others. It also reminds us of the need for ethical discipline.

On these grounds, therefore, I believe that religion is still relevant today. But consider this too: some years ago, the body of a Stone Age man was recovered from the ice of the European Alps. Despite being more than five thousand years old, he was perfectly preserved. Even his clothes were fully intact. I remember thinking at the time that if it were possible to bring this individual back to life for a day, we would find that we have much in common with him. Differences of culture and expression notwithstanding, we would still be able to identify with one another on a basic human level. And there would be no reason to assume that he had any less concern with finding happiness and avoiding suffering than we have. If, religion with its emphasis on overcoming suffering through the practice of ethical discipline and cultivation of love and compassion, can be conceived of as relevant in the past, then we have no grounds to say that it is not equally so today. Granted that in the past, the value of religion may have been more obvious in that human suffering was more explicit due to the lack of modern advantages. But because we humans still suffer, albeit that today this is experienced more internally as mental and emotional affliction, religion with its concern to help us overcome suffering, must still be relevant.

How then might we go about bringing about the harmony that is necessary to overcome inter-religious conflict? As with individuals engaged in the discipline of restraining their response to afflictive emotions and cultivating spiritual qualities, the key lies in developing understanding. We must first identify the factors that obstruct it. Then we must find ways to overcome them.

Perhaps the most significant obstruction to inter-religious harmony is ignorance. Until comparatively recently, communication between different cultures, even different communities, was slow or non-existent. For this reason, sympathy for other faith traditions was not necessarily very important – except of course where members of different religions lived side by side. But this attitude is no longer viable. In today's increasingly complex and interdependent world, we are compelled to acknowledge the existence of other cultures, different ethnic groups and, of course, other religious faiths. Whether we like it or not, most of us now experience this diversity on a daily basis.

I believe the best way to overcome ignorance and bring about understanding is through dialogue with members of other faith traditions. This I see occurring in a number of different ways. Discussions amongst scholars in which the convergence, and perhaps more importantly, the divergence between different faith traditions is explored and appreciated are very valuable. On another level, encounters between ordinary, but practiced followers of different religions in which each share their experiences are helpful. This is perhaps the most effective way of appreciating others' teachings. In my own case, for example, my meetings with the late Thomas Merton, a Catholic monk of the Cistercian order, were deeply inspiring. They helped me develop a profound admiration for the teachings of Christianity. Thirdly, I feel that occasional meetings between religious leaders joining together to pray for a common cause is extremely useful. The gathering at Assisi in Italy where representatives of the world's major religions gathered to pray for peace, was, I believe, tremendously beneficial to many religious believers insofar as it symbolised solidarity and a commitment to peace on the part of all those taking part.

Finally, I feel that the practice of members of different faith traditions going on joint pilgrimages together can be very helpful. It was in this spirit that during 1993 I went to Lourdes and then to Jerusalem, a site holy to three of the world's great religions. I have also paid visits to various Hindu, Islamic, Jain and Sikh shrines both in India and abroad. More recently, following a seminar devoted to discussing and practising meditation in the Christian and Buddhist traditions, I joined an historic pilgrimage of practitioners of both traditions in a programme of prayers, meditation and dialogue under the Bodhi tree at Bodh Gaya in India. This is one of Buddhism's most important shrines.

Where exchanges like these occur, followers of one

tradition will find that, just as in the case of their own, the teachings of other faiths are a source both of spiritual inspiration and of ethical guidance to their followers. It will also become clear that, irrespective of doctrinal and other differences, all the major world religions are concerned with helping individuals to become good human beings. All emphasize love and compassion, patience, tolerance, forgiveness, humility and so on. And all are capable of helping individuals to develop these. Moreover, the example given by the founders of each major religion clearly demonstrates a concern for helping others find happiness through developing these qualities. So far as their own lives were concerned, each conducted themselves with great simplicity. Ethical discipline and love for all others was the hallmark of their lives. They did not live luxuriously like emperors and kings. Instead, they voluntarily accepted suffering – without consideration of the hardships involved – in order to benefit humanity as a whole. In their teachings, all placed special emphasis on developing love and compassion and renouncing selfish desires. Each of them called on us to transform our hearts and minds. Indeed, whether we have faith or not, all are worthy of our profound admiration.

At the same time as engaging in dialogue with followers of other religions we must, of course, implement in our daily life the teachings of our own religion. Once we have experienced the benefit of love and compassion, and of ethical discipline, we will easily recognize the value of others' teachings. But for this, it is essential to realize that religious practice entails a lot more than merely saying 'I believe' or, as in Buddhism, 'I take refuge'. There is also more to it than just visiting temples, or shrines, or churches. Taking religious teachings is of little benefit if they do not enter the heart but remain at the level of intellect alone. Simply relying on faith without understanding and without implementation is of limited value. I often tell Tibetans that carrying a *mala* (something like a rosary) does not make a person a genuine religious practitioner. The efforts we make sincerely to transform ourselves spiritually are what make us genuine religious practitioners.

We come to see the over-riding importance of genuine practice when we recognize that, along with ignorance, individuals' unhealthy relationships with their beliefs is the other major factor in religious disharmony. Far from applying the teachings of our religion in our personal lives, we have a tendency to use them to reinforce our self-centred attitudes. We relate to our religion as to something we own or as a label that distinguishes us from others. Clearly this is misguided. This is to use the nectar of religion not to purify the poisonous elements of our hearts and minds, but rather, to use those negative elements to poison the nectar of religion.

Yet we must acknowledge that this reflects a deeper problem which is implicit in all religions. I refer to the claims each has of being the one 'true' religion. How are we to resolve this difficulty? It is true that from the point of view of the individual practitioner, it is essential to have a single-pointed commitment to our own faith. It is also true that this depends on the deeply felt conviction that our path is the sole mediator of truth. But at the same time, we have to find some means of reconciling this belief with the reality of a multiplicity of similar claims. In practical terms, this involves individual practitioners finding some way to accept the validity of other religions whilst maintaining whole-hearted commitment to their own.

In my own case, I am convinced that Buddhism provides me with the most effective framework within which to situate my efforts to develop spiritually through cultivating love and compassion. At the same time, I must acknowledge that whilst Buddhism represents the best path for me – that is, my character, my temperament, my inclinations and my cultural background – the same will be true of Christianity for Christians. For them, Christianity is the best way. On the basis of my conviction, I cannot therefore say that Buddhism is best for everyone.

I often think of religion in terms of medicine for the human spirit. As with medicine, independent of its usage and suitability to a particular individual in a particular condition, we cannot really judge its efficacy. We are not justified in saying this medicine is very good because of such and such ingredients. If you take the patient and its effect on that person out of the equation it hardly makes sense. What is relevant is to say that in the case of this particular patient with this particular illness, this medicine is the most effective. Similarly with different religious traditions, we can say that this one is most effective for this particular individual. But it is unhelpful to try to argue on the basis philosophy or metaphysics that one religion is 'better' than another. The important thing is its effectiveness in individual cases.

My way to resolve the seeming contradiction between each religion's claim to 'one truth and one religion' and the reality of the multiplicity of faiths is thus to understand that in the case of a single individual, there can be only one truth, one religion. However, from the perspective of human society at large, we must accept the concept of 'many truths, many religions'. To continue with our medical analogy, in the case of one particular patient, the suitable medicine is in fact the only medicine. But clearly that does not mean there may not be other medicines suitable to other patients.

Actually, to my way of thinking, the diversity that exists amongst the various religious traditions is enormously enriching. There is thus no need to try to find ways of saying that ultimately all religions are the same. They are similar in that they all emphasize the indispensability of love and compassion in the context of ethical discipline. But to say this is not to say that they are all essentially one. For example, the contradictory understanding of Creation, on the part of some faith traditions and beginninglessness articulated by others means that in the end we have to part company when it comes to philosophy, in spite of the many practical similarities that undoubtedly exist. These philosophical contradictions may not be very important in the beginning stages of religious practice. But as we advance along the path of one tradition of another, we are compelled at some point to acknowledge fundamental differences. For example, the concept of rebirth in Buddhism and various other ancient Indian traditions is incompatible with the Christian idea of salvation. This need not be a cause for dismay, however. Even within Buddhism itself, in the realm of metaphysics there are diametrically opposing views. At the very least, such diversity means that we have different frameworks within which to locate ethical discipline and the development of spiritual values. That is why I do not advocate a new 'world' or a 'super' religion. It would mean that we would lose the unique characteristics of the different faith traditions.

Some people, it is true, hold that the Buddhist concept of *shunyata*, or emptiness, is ultimately the same as certain approaches to understanding the concept of God. Nevertheless, there remain difficulties with this. The first is that while of course we can interpret these concepts, if we do so to what extent can we be faithful to the original teachings? There are compelling similarities between the Mahayana Buddhist concept of *Dharmakaya*, *Sambogakaya* and *Nirmanakaya* and the Christian Trinity of God as Father, Son and Holy Spirit. But to say, on the basis of this, that Buddhism and Christianity are ultimately the same is to go a bit too far I think! As an old Tibetan saying goes, we must beware of trying to put a yak's head on a sheep's body – or vice versa.

What is required instead is that we develop a genuine sense of religious pluralism. This is especially true if we are serious in our respect for human rights as a universal principle. In this regard, I find the concept of a world parliament of religions very appealing. To begin with, the word 'parliament' conveys a sense of democracy while the plural 'religions' underlines the importance of the principle of a multiplicity of faith traditions. The truly pluralist perspective on religion, which the idea of such a parliament suggests, would, I believe, be beneficial. It would help avoid the extremes of religious bigotry on the one hand, and the urge towards unnecessary syncretism on the other.

Connected with this issue of inter-religious harmony, I should perhaps say something about religious conversion. This is a question which must be taken extremely seriously. To begin with, it is essential to realize that the mere fact of conversion alone will not make an individual a better person – that is to say a more disciplined, a more compassionate and warm-hearted person. Much more helpful, therefore, is for the individual to concentrate on transforming themselves spiritually through the practise of restraint, virtue and compassion. To the extent that the insights or practices of other religions are useful or relevant to our own faith, it is valuable to learn from them. In some cases it may even be helpful to adopt certain of their practices. If this is done wisely, we can remain firmly committed to our own faith. Staying within our own faith is usually best because it carries with it no danger of confusion, especially with respect to the different ways of life that tend to go with different faith traditions.

Given the diversity to be found amongst individual human beings it is of course bound to be the case that out of many millions of practitioners of a particular religion, a handful will come to find that another religion's approach to ethics and spiritual development is more satisfactory. For some, the concept of rebirth and *karma* will come to seem highly effective in inspiring the aspiration to develop love and compassion within the context of responsibility. For others, the concept of a transcendent, loving Creator will come to seem more so. In such circumstances, it is crucial for those individuals to question themselves again and again. They must ask 'Am I attracted to this other religion for the right reasons? Is it merely the cultural and ritual aspects that are appealing? Do I suppose that if I convert to this new religion it will be less demanding than my present one?' I say this because it has often struck me that when people do convert to a religion outside their own heritage, quite often they adopt certain superficial aspects of the culture to which their new faith belongs. But their practice may not go very much deeper than that.

In the case of a person who decides after a process of

long and mature reflection to adopt a different religion, it is very important that they remember the positive contribution to humanity of each religious tradition. The danger is that the individual may feel a need to justify their decision. This can lead in turn to criticism and expressions of dissatisfaction concerning their previous faith. It is essential to avoid this. Just because that tradition is no longer effective in the case of one individual does not mean it is no longer of benefit to humanity. On the contrary, we can be certain that it has been an inspiration to millions of people in the past, that it inspires millions today, and that it will inspire millions in the path of love and compassion in the future.

Ultimately the important point to keep in mind is that the whole purpose of religion is to facilitate love and compassion, patience, tolerance, humility, forgiveness and so on. If we neglect these, changing our religion will be of no help. In the same way, even if we are fervent believers in our own faith, it will avail us nothing if we neglect to implement these qualities in our daily lives. Such a believer is no better off than a patient with a fatal illness who reads a medical treatise but fails to undertake the treatment prescribed.

Moreover, if those of you, who are supposed practitioners of religion, are not compassionate and disciplined, how can we expect it of others? If we can establish genuine harmony derived from mutual respect and understanding, religion has enormous potential to speak with authority on such vital moral questions as peace and disarmament, social and political justice, the natural environment and many other matters affecting all humanity. But until we are seen putting our own spiritual teachings into practice,we will never be taken seriously. And this means, amongst other things, setting a good example through developing good relations with other faith traditions.

AN APPEAL

That we have reached the last few pages of this book reminds us of the impermanence of our lives. How quickly they pass and how soon we will arrive at our final day. Within less than fifty years, I Tenzin Gyatso, the Buddhist monk will be no more than a memory. Indeed, it is doubtful whether a single person reading these words will be alive a century from now. Time passes unhindered. When we make mistakes, we cannot turn the clock back and try again. All we can do is use the present well. Therefore, when our final day comes if we are able to look back and see that we have lived full, productive and meaningful lives, that will at least be of some comfort. If we cannot, we may be very sad. But which of these we experience is up to us.

The best way to ensure that when we approach death we do so without remorse is to ensure that in the present moment we conduct ourselves responsibly and with compassion for others. Actually this is in our own interest. And not just because it will benefit us in the future. As we have seen, compassion is what makes our life meaningful. It is the source of all lasting happiness and joy. And it is the foundation of a good heart, the heart of one who acts out of a desire to help others. Through kindness, through affection, through honesty, through truth and justice towards all others we ensure our own benefit. This is not a matter for complicated theorizing. It is a matter of common sense. There is no denying that consideration of others is worthwhile. There is no denying that our happiness is inextricably bound up with the happiness of others. There is no denying that if society suffers we ourselves suffer. Nor is there any denying that the more our hearts and minds are afflicted with ill will, the more miserable we become. Thus we can reject everything else: religion, ideology, all received wisdom. But we cannot escape the necessity of love and compassion.

This then is my true religion, my simple faith. In this sense, there is no need for temple or church, for mosque or synagogue, no need for complicated philosophy, doctrine or dogma. Our own heart, our own mind is the temple. The doctrine is compassion. Love for others and respect for their rights and dignity, no matter who or what they are: ultimately these are all we need. So long as we practise these in our daily lives then no matter if we are learned or unlearned, whether we believe in Buddha or God or follow some other religion or none at all, so long as we have compassion for others and conduct ourselves with restraint out of a sense of responsibility, there is no doubt we will be happy.

Why then, if it is so simple to be happy do we find it so hard? Unfortunately, though most of us think of ourselves as compassionate, we tend to ignore these common sense truths. We neglect to confront our negative thoughts and emotions. Unlike the farmer who follows the seasons and does not hesitate to cultivate the land when the moment comes, we waste so much of our time in meaningless activity. We feel deep regret over trivial matters like losing money whilst keeping from doing what is genuinely important without the slightest feeling of remorse. Instead of rejoicing in the opportunity we have to contribute to others' well-being, we merely take our pleasures where we can. We shrink from considering others on the grounds that we are too busy. We run right and left, making calculations and telephone calls and thinking that this would be better than that. We do one thing but worry that if something else comes along we had better do another. In doing so, we engage only in the coarsest and most elementary levels of the human spirit. Moreover, by being inattentive to the needs of others, inevitably we end up harming them. We think ourselves very clever, but how do we use our abilities? All too often we use them to deceive our neighbours, to take advantage of them and better ourselves at their expense. And when things do not work out, full of self-righteousness, we blame them for our difficulties.

Yet lasting satisfaction cannot be derived from the acquisition of objects. No matter how many friends we acquire, they cannot make us happy. And sensual pleasure is nothing but a gateway to suffering. It is like honey smeared along the cutting edge of a sword. Of course, that is not to say that we should despise our bodies. On the contrary, we cannot be of help to others without a body. But we need to avoid the extremes to which, all too easily, sensual pleasure leads.

In focusing on the mundane, what is essential remains hidden from us. Of course, if we could be truly happy doing this, then it would be entirely reasonable to live like this. Yet we cannot. At best we get through life without too much trouble. But then when problems assail us, as they must, we are unprepared. We find that we cannot cope. We are left despairing and unhappy.

Therefore, with my two hands joined, I appeal to you the reader, to ensure that you make the rest of your life as meaningful as possible. Do this by engaging in spiritual practice if you can. As I hope I have made clear, there is nothing mysterious in this. It consists in nothing more than acting out of concern for others. And provided you undertake this practice sincerely and with persistence, little by little, step by step you will gradually be able to reorder your habits and attitudes so that you think less about your own narrow concerns and more of others'. In doing so, you will find that you enjoy peace and happiness yourself.

Relinquish your envy, let go your desire to triumph over others. Instead try to benefit them. With kindness, with courage and confident that in doing so you are sure to meet with success, welcome others with a smile. Be straightforward. And try to be impartial. Treat everyone as if they were a close friend. I say this neither as Dalai Lama nor as someone who has special powers or ability. Of these I have none. I speak as a human being: one who, like yourself wishes to be happy and not to suffer.

If you cannot, for whatever reason be of help to others, at least don't harm them. Consider yourself a tourist. Think of our planet as it is seen from space, so small and insignificant yet so beautiful. Could there really be anything to be gained from harming others during our stay here? Is it not preferable, and more reasonable to relax and enjoy ourselves quietly, just as if we were visiting a different neighbourhood? Therefore, if in the midst of your enjoyment of the world you have a moment, try to help in however small a way, those who are downtrodden and those who, for whatever reason, cannot or do not help themselves. Try not to turn away from those whose appearance is disturbing, from the ragged and unwell.

Try never to think of them as inferior to yourself. If you can, try not even to think of yourself as better than the humblest beggar. You will look the same in your grave.

To close with, I would like to share a short prayer which gives me great inspiration in my quest to benefit others:

> May I become at all times, both now and forever
> A protector for those without protection
> A guide for those who have lost their way
> A ship for those with oceans to cross
> A bridge for those with rivers to cross
> A sanctuary for those in danger
> A lamp for those in need of light
> A place of refuge for those in need of shelter.
> And a servant to all those in need.